TRUTH FOR LIFE®

THE BIBLE-TEACHING MINISTRY OF **ALISTAIR BEGG**

The mission of Truth For Life is to teach the Bible with clarity and relevance so that unbelievers will be converted, believers will be established, and local churches will be strengthened.

Daily Program

Each day, Truth For Life distributes the Bible teaching of Alistair Begg across the U.S. and in several locations outside of the U.S. through 1,800 radio outlets. To find a radio station near you, visit **truthforlife. org/stationfinder**.

Free Teaching

The daily program, and Truth For Life's entire teaching archive of over 2,000 Bible-teaching messages, can be accessed for free online and through Truth For Life's full-feature mobile app. Download the free mobile app at **truthforlife.org/app** and listen free online at **truthforlife.org**.

At-Cost Resources

Books and full-length teaching from Alistair Begg on CD, DVD, and USB are available for purchase at cost, with no markup. Visit **truthforlife.org/store**.

Where to Begin?

If you're new to Truth For Life and would like to know where to begin listening and learning, find starting point suggestions at **truthforlife. org/firststep**. For a full list of ways to connect with Truth For Life, visit **truthforlife.org/subscribe**.

Contact Truth For Life

P.O. Box 398000 Cleveland, Ohio 44139

phone 1 (888) 588-7884   **email** letters@truthforlife.org

/truthforlife   @truthforlife   truthforlife.org

OUR
ANCIENT
FOE

OUR ANCIENT FOE

Satan's History,
Activity, and
Ultimate Demise

Edited by Ronald L. Kohl

P&R
PUBLISHING
P.O. BOX 817 • PHILLIPSBURG • NEW JERSEY 08865-0817

Unless otherwise indicated, Scripture quotations are from the ESV® Bible (The Holy Bible, English Standard Version®), copyright © 2001 by Crossway, a publishing ministry of Good News Publishers. Used by permission. All rights reserved.

The New Testament in Modern English by J.B Phillips copyright © 1960, 1972 J. B. Phillips. Administered by The Archbishops' Council of the Church of England. Used by permission.

Unless otherwise indicated, Scripture quotations in chapter 7 are taken from the King James Version.

Italics within Scripture quotations indicate emphasis added.

Chapter 1 is based on *Genesis* by R. Kent Hughes, © 2004. Used by permission of Crossway, a publishing ministry of Good News Publishers, Wheaton, IL 60187, www.crossway.org.

Chapter 6 is based on *Ephesians* by R. Kent Hughes, © 1990. Used by permission of Crossway, a publishing ministry of Good News Publishers, Wheaton, IL 60187, www.crossway.org.

Printed in the United States of America

ISBN: 978-1-62995-645-9 (pbk)
ISBN: 978-1-62995-646-6 (ePub)
ISBN: 978-1-62995-647-3 (Mobi)

Library of Congress Cataloging-in-Publication Data has been applied for and is available with the Library of Congress.

Contents

Editor's Preface

THIS IS a book about our adversary—the enemy of our souls. He goes by many names: Satan. The devil. The accuser of the brethren. The serpent of old. Beelzebub. Some are descriptive titles; some are names. This is a book that I pray will fill a valuable role in the realm of Christian literature, for I fear there are far too few trustworthy resources that speak of our enemy, the devil. The Bible speaks often and definitely about Satan's person and work. Sometimes it speaks via allusions or references; sometimes Scripture mentions him by name.

I fear that, as Christians, we take Satan far too lightly. The Bible tells us in 1 Peter 5:8 that, as our enemy, the devil "prowls around like a roaring lion, seeking someone to devour." And yet we are so often caught off guard, easily deceived, and ignorant of his plans, power, and presence. Wilhelmus à Brakel, the great Dutch theologian of the late seventeenth and early eighteenth centuries, said, "Most of the time the devil conceals himself and seeks to convince man that he has no hand in what transpired, but rather that it is the person himself and that such things proceed from his own heart. Thereby he seeks either to prevent that which is good and to corrupt it, to bring about the commission of sin, or to bring the soul into a state of bewilderment."[1]

1. Wilhelmus à Brakel, *The Christian's Reasonable Service*, vol. 4, *Ethics and Eschatology*, trans. Bartel Elshout, ed. Joel R. Beeke (Grand Rapids:

Satan is a very real person, and his presence can be felt if we are sensitive to such things. I spent some time in remote areas of Tanzania in 2007. One of the villages that we visited revealed a deep heaviness as soon as we entered it. It's hard to describe, but I felt a tangible dark weight that didn't dissipate until we left its borders. Many years later, I described the presence to a pastor friend of mine who had spent twelve years as a missionary to the same Tanzanian people group. As soon as I started to describe it, he immediately identified what village it was. He had experienced the same demonic presence I had.

I don't claim to be an expert of any sort, but I have been called upon, once or twice, to minister to brothers and sisters who were dealing with spiritual oppression. I go into situations like that with great fear and trembling. I don't want to discount or underestimate the enemy. At the same time, I don't want to overestimate Satan or his servants, for he is a defeated foe. But when it comes to the enemy of our souls, wariness is essential to our resistance. May this book be a tool in the hands of Christian believers of all sorts—pastors and laypersons alike.

I have had the great privilege of sitting at the feet of spiritual giants, many of whose writings appear here. I recall attending the Philadelphia Conference on Reformed Theology for the first time—more years ago than I can remember. Every pew in Philadelphia's venerable Tenth Presbyterian Church was filled, and from the time that the late Dr. James Montgomery Boice stepped to the pulpit, I was hooked. I know that each man who spoke was just a humble servant of the Word, but the authority of that Word, in the hands of gifted teachers, gripped me from the start.

Reformation Heritage Books, 1995), available online at https://biblical spirituality.files.wordpress.com/2010/03/reasonableservicevol4-indexed .pdf, p. 237.

Several of the chapters in this work began as plenary messages at the 2017 Quakertown (PA) Conference on Reformed Theology, which I have had the privilege of chairing since its inception in 2008 as a partnered event with the Alliance of Confessing Evangelicals. It was through the Alliance that I first learned about and was able to attend PCRT, and our conference, which is held at the church that I serve as pastor—Grace Bible Fellowship Church in Quakertown—is a by-product of the Alliance's efforts.

Each year, as I seek to introduce and develop a conference theme that will be beneficial to those who attend, I intentionally try to focus on the practical. I ask myself, "What do attendees need to hear? What will help them in their walk with Christ? What will give them ammunition as they seek to live as shining lights in a dark world?" "For Still Our Ancient Foe" came to mind as a theme for 2017, and Alliance executive director Robert Brady was immediately and enthusiastically supportive.

The Alliance graciously granted me access to the vast vaults of PCRT messages from 1974–2017 as I sought to develop a full-orbed work that more or less chronologically deals with the devil as he appears in Scripture, and I am delighted and humbled that they encouraged me to contribute a chapter myself. The four chapters attributed to R. Kent Hughes and Tom Nettles were delivered at QCRT, and four chapters were first delivered in Philadelphia. I tried to select material for this volume based on frequently asked questions: Who is the devil? How did he become our sworn enemy? What are his methods? What are his intentions? How do we stand against him? What does his future hold?

In addition to the fine offerings by Drs. Hughes and Nettles, I am thankful for this volume's other contributors, starting with the late Roger Nicole and also including Joel Beeke,

Sinclair Ferguson, and Derek Thomas. The editing process was a largely delightful one because of the richness of the content supplied by these brilliant pastor-theologians as they worked through a number of themes and texts. Many of the primary Scriptures concerning our adversary are exposited here, such as Genesis 3, Luke 22, Ephesians 2, Ephesians 6, Colossians 3, Revelation 20, and Revelation 21. It is my desire that readers will find this book helpful, practical, and encouraging.

A number of sincere and heartfelt thank-yous are in order, starting with the church family whom I have the distinct privilege of serving as pastor. To the folks at Grace Bible Fellowship Church: I am so very grateful for the opportunity to stand before you week after week, armed with the inerrant, infallible, authoritative Word of God, and to proclaim that Word before a receptive, eager audience who accept no substitutes. QCRT depends on the faithfulness and enthusiasm of the many who volunteer their time and talents; many who serve have helped every year since our conference's inception. I'm thankful for the elders and deacons here at Grace, and for the teamwork and camaraderie of assistant pastor Tim Radcliff and youth minister Cory Arnold.

I am grateful to Bob Brady, Jeff Mindler, Ben Ciavolella, and the friendly staff at the Alliance of Confessing Evangelicals for their friendship and encouragement, both with QCRT and with this book project. Thanks as well to P&R Publishing, both for the honor of allowing me to edit a second book (you'd think they would have learned their lesson after the first one, *The Triune God*) and for the privilege of supplying a chapter. I so very greatly appreciate the steady stream of encouragement offered by Bryce Craig and Ian Thompson of P&R, and I'm thankful to Aaron Gottier and Amanda Martin for their patience and insights. I have learned a great deal about editing from these fine people!

QCRT has allowed me some amazing opportunities to partner with speakers who have graciously given of themselves to offer wise counsel and to sacrifice time at home in order to travel to our small town. You have reminded me how important it is to take time to help others in ministry, even though you're all so very, very busy. Your assistance has instilled in me a desire to "pay it forward."

I've been blessed to have a denomination, the Bible Fellowship Church, that has fostered and encouraged my writing over these many years. Beyond that, great men like Carl C. Cassel, Clifford B. Boone, Randall A. Grossman, and Ronald C. Mahurin have provided godly examples worthy of emulation. Thank you, brothers! I am also personally grateful to a coterie of pastor-friends who have lifted my spirits time and time again.

Finally, to Kendra, my dear wife: you are better than I deserve. You show me God's matchless grace through your love, your laughter, and your support. I more fully understand the wonderful Ephesians 5 metaphor of Christ's love for his church through your love for your husband.

Soli Deo gloria!

Ronald L. Kohl

1

Satan in the Garden

R. KENT HUGHES

Genesis 3:1–7

IN GENESIS 3 we find Adam and Eve living in unparalleled splendor amid the green forests of Eden, in perfect harmony with the birds of the air and the beasts of the field. And this magnificent couple shared a profound harmony of soul—they were of the same bone and flesh. Eve was Adam's daughter, in the sense that she came out of him. Eve was also Adam's sister, because they shared the same father. And Eve was Adam's one-flesh wife! What they experienced in the beginning reflected the eternal glory and order of the Trinity, and it ultimately foreshadowed the intimacy of Christ with his church. Paul would quote Genesis 2:24 in Ephesians 5:31–32:

> "Therefore a man shall leave his father and mother and hold
> fast to his wife, and the two shall become one flesh." This

mystery is profound, and I am saying that it refers to Christ and the church.

Adam and Eve's union was glorious. From the beginning, it gave substantial glory to God.

We must note that Adam's headship and authority were part of creation before sin and the fall—before anything wicked had entered the picture. Adam's headship was evident for four reasons. Obviously, he was created first. Paul makes that a central fact in his argument about creation order in 1 Timothy 2:13: "For Adam was formed first, then Eve." Next, we note that Eve was taken out of man, which Paul likewise uses in a similar argument in 1 Corinthians 11:8: "For man was not made from woman, but woman from man." We note, third, that Eve was designated as Adam's "helper," whereas this could not be said of Adam in respect to Eve. Lastly, Genesis 2 and 3 rest on the careful creation order of God, man, woman, and the beasts (in Genesis 3, the serpent). This order was tragically reversed by the fall, when the woman listened to the serpent, the man listened to the woman—and no one listened to God.

Naked and Not Ashamed

This sinless pair nestled on the pinnacle of innocence and openness. Genesis 2:25 reads, "The man and his wife were both naked and were not ashamed." They were spiritually naked before God; God came first in love and first in their thoughts, as C. S. Lewis noted, "without painful effort."[1] It

1. C. S. Lewis, *The Problem of Pain* (repr., San Francisco: Harper San Francisco, 2001), 74.

was just there. There was no need for disciplined devotion; all of life was devotion! Loving God was as natural as breathing and as effortless. Sounds like heaven to me. And it will be.

Adam and Eve were naked with each other. Clothing had never occurred to them. There was nothing to hide, nothing to protect. There was no gravitational pull of "self." They were not self-centered but other-centered. They were directed outwardly toward God and toward each other, and in all this, they were simply there for each other to see and love. You could say, in concert with that beautiful line from Shakespeare's *Merchant of Venice*, that Eve was placed in Adam's "constant soul," as he was in hers.[2] They were both naked in their environment, ecologically at home in the garden, and in harmony with its beasts—naked and unashamed.

Note that Genesis 2:25–3:7 should be taken as a unit—both ends of this section focus on the couple's nakedness, but with radically different contexts. Whereas 2:25 pictures Adam and Eve at the pinnacle of innocence and intimacy, 3:7 describes them in the pit of guilt and estrangement as they hide their nakedness. What we have in this section is a description of the couple's descent from innocence to guilt under the guile of the Prince of Darkness Grim—Satan himself. You see it here in one step after another. As primal history, this describes what has happened countless times down through the ages, and so what we have here is universal. This is for all people, and everyone needs to listen well if they are to resist this Prince of Darkness. Everyone needs to hear this.

This passage can be understood in two sections. First, in Genesis 3:1–5, we hear the dialogue that leads to the descent

---

2. "And true she is, as she hath proved herself, and therefore, like herself, wise, fair, and true, shall she be placed in my constant soul" (William Shakespeare, *The Merchant of Venice*, act 2, scene 6, lines 57–59).

of Adam and Eve. Next, in verses 6–7, we see them descend into the pit. The surprise in all of this is that the initiator of the dialogue is a talking snake. Now, we know that it is not a bad snake, because everything that God created was good. I have to say it: I don't like snakes. Snakes as a species carry an almost entirely negative connotation. But at this point, before the fall, sin had made no entrance into the world. The snake itself eventually acts like a bad snake, but it is just a snake. And its description as "crafty" or "shrewd" does not imply that it is evil. That is just how a snake is: wary, knowing where the dangers lurk. This is a naturally shrewd creature, but under the control of Satan it becomes a natural tool for evil. The New Testament identifies the serpent as the devil (see Rev. 12:9; 20:2)—so we know that the devil is using this snake.

The scene itself raises some interesting questions. We are told that the serpent is one of the wild animals that the Lord has made. Perhaps it was not common in the garden; maybe that is why Eve did not run in terror when the snake began to speak. I wonder, did the snake suddenly drop from a tree? Did he extend himself upright so he could address Eve, tongue to forked tongue? "Good morning, fair lady. Mind if I recoil here a while?" Did it hiss or lisp its words, or did it perhaps speak with a voice like Eve's husband? We do not know, but there is one thing we do know: right here in the beginning, in the primeval event that led to the fall, the serpent attacked God's Word.

Remember that Genesis begins with God creating everything by his Word. He spoke, and it was so. He spoke, and out came the sun and the moon. He spoke, and there was the dappled blue sky. He spoke, and there was the exotic garden, the flowers, the singing birds, the adoring creatures. He spoke, and there was Adam. All came from God's good Word—God's speech, his word, his revelation . . . which Satan now attacks.

Satan Attacks

Satan's attack opened with a question in a surprised, incredulous tone: "Did God actually say, 'You shall not eat of *any* tree in the garden'?" (v. 1). The devil was consummately shrewd—for, while he did not directly deny God's Word, he smuggled in the implication that God's Word is subject to human judgment. Such a thought had never been verbalized to Eve. She had never imagined that she could judge God's Word for herself. Now such a prospect was offered to her, and she found the offer alluring.

The serpent, shrewd as he was and is, also avoided the use of God's covenant name—Yahweh, the LORD. It's fascinating that in Genesis 1, where we see God creating, *Elohim* is the name used in every reference to him. But, in chapters 2–4, his title changes to *Yahweh Elohim*, which combines both the creator and the covenant names of God—everywhere except for the dialogue in these opening verses of chapter 3, where the text reverts to *Elohim*, the more remote designation for God. Ominously, when Eve refers to him, she uses *Elohim* as well. Our ancient foe was at work. Satan's incredulous tone and his premeditated refusal to use God's personal name set up his studied distortion of God's Word.

Remember that the Lord God had generously commanded, "You may surely eat of every tree of the garden, but of the tree of the knowledge of good and evil you shall not eat" (Gen. 2:16–17). Every tree of the garden, save one, was for food. Now Satan asked, "Did God [*Elohim*] actually say, 'You shall not eat of *any* tree in the garden'?" He assaulted God's generosity—the creator God and all that he had given. The Prince of Darkness Grim was so subtle that Eve did not have the slightest notion of what was going on. His question seemed like an innocent one, but the seed of doubt concerning

5

God's Word had been planted in Eve's heart, and it would bear immediate, tragic fruit.

When the snake posed his infamous, deceit-filled question, Eve had an opportunity to set him straight. But she failed. Instead, she added her own revisions to God's Word—three sad distortions through which she first diminished God's Word, then added to God's Word, and then softened his Word. How so? First, as we have seen, God had said, "You may surely eat of every tree of the garden." But now Eve leaves out the word *every*. She simply says, "We may eat of the fruit of the trees in the garden" (Gen. 3:2). Her inexact, bland rendition of God's Word discounted and shrank his generosity. Eve was, at the very least, unconsciously nodding in agreement with the serpent, and an ominous shift was happening in her heart.

Second, Eve further revealed her subtle shift in heart by adding to God's Word. We read her saying, at the beginning of verse 3: "But God [Elohim] said, 'You shall not eat of the fruit of the tree that is in the midst of the garden, neither shall you touch it.'" Satan was having his way with Eve. God had never forbidden touching the fruit. Eve magnified God's strictness, insinuating that he was so harsh that an inadvertent slip would bring death. This is typical of the sons and daughters of Eve. Imagine the boss who calls an employee because he has been late several times and who says to the employee, "You know, I think this is a habit you need to change." The employee walks out of the office and says to his coworkers, "You know what that stuffed shirt said? If I'm late again, I'm fired." When we dislike a prohibition or warning, we magnify its strictness with additions that make it sound unreasonable. An alarm should sound inside our heads when we begin to think that God's Word is unreasonable or that it requires too much.

Finally, Eve softens the warning of God's Word by saying merely, "Lest you die," instead of, "Lest you *surely* die." This removed the certitude of God's declaration. Eve, in a mere breath, under Satan's sway, diminished the Word, added to the Word, and softened the Word. Her revisionist handling of God's holy Word put her in harm's way, as it does for us today when we do the same. She also emboldened Satan to make a heinous claim, as we see in Genesis 3:4: "But the serpent said to the woman, 'You will *not* surely die.'" What an in-your-face, blasphemous statement about God's Word this was. The Hebrew takes the world *lo* (not) and places it first in front of God's declaration, so that it literally says, "*Not* you shall surely die." It is now the serpent's word against God's—an absurd juxtaposition. Eve should have recoiled and run screaming to Adam. And Adam should have stepped forth to uphold the good Word of God. But Eve was buying it. She was entranced by the serpent—flushed with excitement over what would go on to consume her.

God's Goodness Questioned

Satan goes even further, attacking the goodness of God himself as he declares in verse 5, "For God knows that when you eat of it"—that is, the tree—"your eyes will be opened, and you will be like God, knowing good and evil." According to the serpent, the threat of death was nothing more than a scare tactic to keep Adam and Eve in place. The implication is clear: God is repressive and jealous, says Satan. God wants to keep Adam and Eve down. What an incredible assault on God's character, in the midst of a garden that was a testament to his cosmic goodness—and Eve is buying it.

For Eve, the lie bore the lure of divinity. Satan told her,

"You will be like God." Such lies have an intrinsic spiritual lure—the promise of ascent and God-like elevation to another world. If you are in the thrall of sin, you will see God's prohibitions as barriers—as obstacles to be climbed by "strong people" like yourself. With enough resolve, Eve could reach out and take that fruit, and divinity would be hers. The lie held out the lure of moral autonomy. She would become wise—become equal with God. She would autonomously decide what was right and wrong. God would no longer tell her what to do. *She* would make the rules. She would do it *her* way. This was an intoxicating promise, and it remains so to this day. Frank Sinatra's "My Way" is a funeral favorite, and we can see why. Its lyrics, about facing and doing everything your way, are the lyrics of autonomy—the dirge of death.

So during the dialogue of descent, Satan attacked God's Word and then God's goodness, and Eve stood still for it. Naked, lovely, sinless, perfect Eve was standing on the abyss.

Standing on the Abyss

The serpent then departs from our view, and Moses, the author of Genesis (as the New Testament tells us numerous times), provides a brilliant picture for us in Genesis 3:6. There is no dialogue; just Eve's thoughts. There is no music here; only silence—and the camera adjusts to slow motion as she "saw that the tree was good for food." It was appealing, a delight to the eyes, and it was to be desired to make one wise. That was the great enticement: wisdom apart from God's Word. Wisdom apart from God.

In that silence, the prospect of God-like moral autonomy ineluctably drew her. God's command for her not to partake of the tree seemed insubstantial. She took its fruit and ate, seeing no reason not to. Moses, the narrator, expresses no shock here. The unthinkable and terrible is described by him as simply and unsensationally as possible. Her action was so natural, so undramatic. "She took of its fruit and ate."

But what she did was cosmic in effect. John Milton, thinking of Romans 8, in which the creation groans, wrote,

> Earth felt the wound; and Nature from her seat,
> Sighing through all her works, gave signs of woe,
> That all was lost.[3]

With Eve's sin committed, the narrative now quickens with a rapid succession of verbs in verse 6: "She took of its fruit and ate, and she also gave some to her husband who was with her, and he ate." Anything shocking there? The shock is that Adam was there for the *entire* episode, listening to the conversation. The text indicates that Adam was "with her." One could possibly say that this does not prove that Adam was with her the whole time—except that throughout the entire account in verses 1–5, when Eve is addressed, she is always addressed *in the plural*. Adam was indeed with her. He was passively watching everything. And he himself was not deceived. His powers of reasoning and perception had been honed by the naming of the animals. He had been through a rigorous intellectual process as he named all of creation. He had probed the essence of each animal and given it a name. Adam was no rustic; his mental powers, said Augustine, surpassed those of the most brilliant philosophers as much as the speed of a bird surpasses a tortoise.[4]

---

3. John Milton, *Paradise Lost*, bk. 9, lines 782–84.
4. Quoted in C. S. Lewis, *A Preface to Paradise Lost* (London: Oxford University Press, 1942), 113.

Listen to what the apostle Paul says in 1 Timothy 2:14: "Adam was not deceived, but the woman was deceived." Adam sinned *willfully*—eyes wide open without hesitation—and his sin was fraught with self-interest. He had watched in fascination as Eve took the fruit. Would she die? Now there's a loving man! And when she ate, and he saw that there were no consequences, he took and ate. Eve followed the snake, Adam followed Eve, and no one followed God. The event was seismic.

Again Milton puts it so beautifully:

Earth trembled from her entrails, as again
In pangs; and Nature gave a second groan;
Sky lowered; and, muttering thunder, some sad drops
Wept at completing of the mortal sin
Original.[5]

Into the Pit

Creation raining cosmic tears—that is the picture we have here. Adam and Eve had fallen from the pinnacle of innocence and intimacy into the pit of guilt and estrangement, as Genesis 3:7 so memorably depicts: "Then the eyes of both were opened, and they knew that they were naked. And they sewed fig leaves together and made themselves loincloths."

What Satan had told them was true . . . *half* true. They did not die that day. In fact, Adam lived 930 years. Yet Adam and Eve did die. Their constant communion with God died. Their eyes were grotesquely opened as they received the knowledge that they sought. They saw evil, and they saw themselves

5. Milton, *Paradise Lost*, bk. 9, lines 1000–1004.

as naked, so that they desperately sought to cover themselves. Their innocence was no more. Guilt and fear gripped their hearts. Now love—loving God and loving each other—would become a labor.

We must not be blind to Satan's schemes, "for we are not ignorant of his designs" (2 Cor. 2:11). The temptation that he effected in Eden is his primary tactic. Genesis is packed with primary wisdom in this regard. From Adam and Eve's sin we learn that sin takes hold when we begin to doubt God's Word.

Doubt about God's Word births biblical revisionism—both consciously and subconsciously. We begin to minimize Scripture's promises through a less-than-enthusiastic rehearsal of its benefits. We discount God's largesse; our colorless renditions of God's glories dim their polychrome wonders, and we feel justified in ignoring his Word.

Not only do we minimize his Word, but we exaggerate what we dislike by adding to his Word. His commands become absurd caricatures that no one expects to obey because they are so requiring, and we count ourselves as being off the hook as far as having to obey them.

Our minimizing and adding to God's Word then leave us free to subtract from his Word. Its teaching about purity and sensuality is considered to be just a product of its culture and irrelevant to moderns (or postmoderns) like us. The Bible is jettisoned in favor of materialism in business. Ultimately, the minimizing, adding, and subtracting leave us without the Word—leave us free-falling into temptation—and then we doubt God's goodness. And, when we doubt God's goodness, the bottom comes up fast!

Let us step back for a moment and reflect. Moses, as the author of the Torah (the Pentateuch—the first five books of the Bible, from Genesis to Deuteronomy) penned the account of the fall in Genesis 3 to show how it was perpetrated by the

Prince of Darkness's attack on God's Word. Moses's warning and call is to make God's Word the center of our existence. Significantly, at the end of the book of Deuteronomy, after Moses has written a copy of the Torah and laid it next to the ark, he sings a song (the Song of Moses). And when he comes to the end of the song, he adds this epilogue: "Take to heart all the words by which I am warning you today, that you may command them to your children, that they may be careful to do all the words of this law. For it is no empty word for you, but your very life" (Deut. 32:46–47).

"Your very life" indicates the regard that those under the old covenant, in the Old Testament, were to hold for Scripture. It was to be regarded as "your very life." We see that Psalm 1, which informs all the other Psalms, begins,

> Blessed is the man
> > who walks not in the counsel of the wicked,
> nor stands in the way of sinners,
> > nor sits in the seat of scoffers;
> but his delight is in the law of the LORD,
> > and on his law he meditates day and night. (vv. 1–2)

Psalm 19 amplifies this point. Its first six verses teach us about how God speaks through creation (through natural revelation), and then its author, David, goes on to describe God's written Word (his special revelation) as being sweeter than honey (see v. 10) and as reviving the soul (see v. 7). And then, of course, there's Psalm 119—a 176-verse Hebrew acrostic poem of 22 stanzas that unfolds according to the 22 letters of the Hebrew alphabet, essentially saying that God's Word is everything from *aleph* to *tau*, or A to Z. And when we come to the end of Isaiah, we read, "But this is the one to whom I will look: he who is humble and contrite in spirit and trembles at my word" (Isa. 66:2). Faithful men and women believed and lived out the fact that God's Word was their very life.

Rescued by the Second Adam

When we come to the New Testament, we come to Jesus Christ, who is at once the second Adam and the second Moses. Jesus's mind encompassed the whole Old Testament. Scholars will say that his allusions come from virtually every book in the Old Testament—that Jesus was full of the Scriptures. And not only that; he lived in full submission to them. "His whole will," says Adolf Schlatter, "was consumed with this: to do what each commandment commanded. Here is the one man—the first in history—who not only knew the Word but did it."[6]

Jesus, as the second Adam and second Moses, knew his Bible; so it is not surprising that when he was answering his critics, he would say, "Have you not read . . . ?" (Matt. 19:4; Mark 12:10; Luke 6:3), or "Have you never read . . . ?" (Matt. 21:16, 42), or "What did Moses command you?" (Mark 10:3). He was fully dependent upon the Word of God. Add to this all his allusions to Scripture and you begin to see that it formed the warp and woof of Jesus's mind. He *did* meditate day and night upon God's Word; he *was* the man of Psalm 1.

Unlike the first Adam, when Jesus was tempted, he threw himself on God's Word, defeating Satan with three deft quotations from Deuteronomy. One of them, recorded in Matthew 4:4 and partially in Luke 4:4, is this: "Man shall not live by bread alone, but by every word that comes from the mouth of

6. Adolf Schlatter, *Das Evangelium nach Matthäus* (repr., Berlin: Evangelische Verlagsanstalt, 1961), 61; quoted in Frederick Dale Bruner, *Matthew: A Commentary*, vol. 1, *The Christbook: Matthew 1–12*, rev. ed. (Grand Rapids: Eerdmans, 2007), 198.

God" (see also Deut. 8:3). The Word is our food; the Word is our life; the Word is *everything* for us.

If we are to resist the temptation of the Prince of Darkness Grim, we must hold fast to God's Word as our very life, as did the first Moses; and then, like Jesus—the second Moses—we must understand that it is our very food.

2

Knowing Satan

THOMAS J. NETTLES

John 10:7–15

THE TITLE of this chapter is "Knowing Satan." You probably know him pretty well already, and likely even have some personal acquaintance with him, at least in his role as tempter and deceiver. But it always helps us to have a precise understanding of exactly who this Prince of Darkness Grim is and exactly what he does when he engages us in our minds and in our affections. It is important to understand that our knowledge of Satan should not simply come through our despair and doubts; we can learn from the Word of God what he is doing. The eruption of our sinful desires, and the envies and jealousies that assault us, almost without any forethought, are all the result of our own lust and our own sinfulness—and yet they fall in such ready line with Satan's will for us. If we can learn how he operates, and how the Scripture depicts him as operating, it will help us as we seek to stand in the face of temptation.

15

Martin Luther, as much as anyone, correctly grasped Satan's presence and methods of operation. Luther said that the greatest punishment that God can inflict on the wicked is leaving them in the hands of Satan—who, when the church delivers the wicked over to him in order to chastise them, makes them undergo great calamities or even kills them. Luther declares, "Many devils are in woods, in waters, in wildernesses, and in dark pooly places, ready to hurt and prejudice people; some are also in the thick black clouds, which cause hail, lightnings, and thunderings, and poison the air, the pastures and grounds."[1]

While Luther's understanding of Satan was greatly influenced by his massive knowledge of Scripture, I think his beliefs also included some holdover from medieval superstitions. Yet that does not mean we should minimize the reality of what he is saying here—that there is an evil influence that is pervasive in the world. We cannot go anyplace in this present world that is not, to some extent and in some way, under the influence of Satan and his angels. There are some societies that are more susceptible to this because they lack the truth. We see Satan's influence somewhat repressed in other places—sometimes because of those societies' heritage of truth and sometimes because they have brilliantly received and accepted the truth. Satan hates the truth and can often be thwarted when the truth is present. But Luther's conviction that Satan seeks to inhabit all places is something that we should take very seriously.

1. *The Table Talk or Familiar Discourse of Martin Luther*, trans. William Hazlitt (London, 1848), 247.

The Foe of God

And so we look now at our Ancient Foe. First, I think we should see him as the foe of God. In Luke 10, after Jesus sent his disciples on a mission trip, they came back having experienced great success, exhilarated with the various things they had been able to do in their preaching and their healing and their casting out of demons. They returned rejoicing that even the devils were subject to them. Jesus then said, "I saw Satan fall like lightning from heaven" (Luke 10:18). I do not think that Jesus was saying, "In your mission trip, as you were casting out demons, I saw the demise of Satan and I saw him falling from heaven." I think he was rather saying, "Be careful about the things that you rejoice in. Be careful about your display of power. Be careful about rejoicing in those things that show that you have some degree of superiority over the forces of this world. This is a voice I've heard before. I saw Satan fall like lightning from heaven. I saw pride come into the highest of all the angels. I saw pride and resistance come into the one who is the most excellent of all the created beings, and there was a truth that he knew about—a truth that wormed its way into his eventual desire for intellectual autonomy and caused him to fight against the very will of God."

Well, what was that truth? Jesus mentions it in verse 20: "Nevertheless, do not rejoice in this, that the spirits are subject to you, but rejoice that your names are written in heaven." Jesus said they should rejoice in unconditional election—that before the foundation of the world, God had placed his love and his grace and his affection upon them.

In verse 21, Jesus says he is thankful that God has hidden these things from the wise and the prudent—those who see themselves as having worldly wisdom and as being able to organize all the intellectual thoughts of the day. These are the ones who do not come to a humble understanding and a humble grasp of the gospel of our Lord Jesus Christ—the substitutionary atonement and the grace of God upon which we are utterly dependent for salvation. God has not revealed this to the wise and the prudent, but he revealed these things to babes. This is what seemed good in the sight of the Father.

Satan was somehow, it seems, privy to this doctrine of unconditional election. Jesus was peculiarly joyful at the thought of this doctrine, but Satan became peculiarly revolted. How could this be? This doctrine involved elevating these new intellectual creatures, who appeared inferior, above Satan. Satan was now going to be a servant. God makes his angels servants of those who are to inherit salvation (see Heb. 1:14). How can this be?

Before his fall, Satan had no internal antagonism to God. He was good, he was beautiful, he was powerful. But as he reasoned his way through this doctrine, it did not make sense to him.[2] The doctrine insulted the understanding that he had of his high position and of the order of intelligent beings. Perhaps Satan reasoned, "This is not like something God would do; there is an order of creation that must be followed. There is an incongruence—a senselessness about making me, an excellent being, and then having these inferior beings above me." And Satan, perhaps knowing some elements of the redemption covenant, thought, "They will become like the Son of God? How can that be?"

I do not know how this line of thinking led to revolution, but we know that it *did* lead to revolution and that Satan was cast out of heaven. And in his response to God's elevation of

2. I recognize that I am somewhat speculating here—though I think I am doing so in light of Scripture, connecting several passages and the particular ways in which we know Satan operates.

man over him, which he looked upon as unnatural, irrational, an insult to his exalted position, Satan put his own rationality in place of God's decree. It began as a rational reticence, but the more Satan thought about everything (outside the context of what God actually was saying about it), the more offensive it all became to him.

In this argument, in this rebellion, in this rejection of divine sovereignty (and particularly the divine sovereignty expressed within the covenant of redemption to save human creatures and make them to be like the Son), Satan fell. His intellectual autonomy resulted in a resistance to the will of God, then resulted in a disaffection from the beauty and glory of God. Satan was cast out—set within a condition of hatred for God, holiness, grace, and goodness. He had come now to steal, to kill, to destroy; he became the wolf that would tear the sheep and everything related to God's purpose. He would now oppose.

Ironically, Satan's rebellion against God was instrumental in God's own decree. The covenant of redemption comes in light of the fall. It comes in light of the necessity of the Son of God's taking to himself our nature and bearing our sin on his own body on the tree. It is made necessary by the operation of the Spirit—his operation of changing our hearts and changing our corruption. All those things that are related, the glories of the gospel of redemption, come into play as a result of Satan's rebellion against God and his purposes. God wisely used Satan's leap into intellectual autonomy, which became a disaffection from the purposes of God, to accomplish his eternal purpose of redemption.

When we begin to allow our thinking to lead us away from absolute obedience to the Word of God, we are misusing our reason and misplacing our affections. There is an eternal logic to the decrees of God, to the revelation of God—one that enables us to connect the dots and make a doctrine out of all these various propositions of Scripture. We are obligated to do so—but if our connecting of the dots somehow leads us away from the plain word of Scripture and the propositional revelation that God has given us, then we are connecting the dots in the wrong way and are putting ourselves on the edge of disobedience to God and disbelief in his Word.

We recognize that there is a consistency within revelation. This is the very thing that supports the work of systematic theology, and we realize that this consistency extends throughout the entire corpus of Scripture. The more Scriptures we have and can synthesize about a particular doctrine, the more accurate our understanding will be. But if we begin to place things within the doctrine that are contradictory to any of the propositions with which we have to deal, then we are setting ourselves on a road toward denial of the Word of God. And often this begins with the idea that some of the things that are revealed just do not seem to fit the way we perceive God's character. "Surely God would not do something so immoral as to place the sins of creatures he has made on his beloved Son and make him a propitiation. What kind of an example is that? That is a justification of child abuse!" So our reasoning goes.

We think that we are doing God a favor; we think we are defending the character of God by denying a plain revelation. When our rationality begins to operate independently of divine revelation, when it opposes the clearly revealed propositions of Scripture, we have fallen into the error of the first opponent of God's infinite wisdom—Satan.

This is the way Satan operates—the method by which he reasoned himself out of heaven. This is the method by which he moved away from being one who looked at God, saw his beauty, and loved his beauty—one who was exhilarated at his presence and felt tremendous privilege in his own exulted position. That is the kind of being that Satan had been, but he fell from that—*not* originally because of a disaffection toward God but because of a sliver of intellectual autonomy. He thought, "This really cannot be what God is going to do."

The Foe of God's Image Bearers

Because Satan is the foe of God, the second thing we need to know about him is that he is also the foe of God's *image bearers*. I need offer only a few suggestions about how a pure heart like Eve's—the heart of one who had walked with God and loved him and saw his beauty and appreciated everything about him, and who had the law written in her heart—actually came to sin.

In our present fallen condition, we know that our affections are corrupt and depraved and that they lead us to sin. They will rule over our rationality and over our will, so that we do what our affections and self-love would have us do. But Eve was not in that condition. She was not yet fallen—and so how did a person who was, as yet, incorrupt sin? What was the manner that brought her to sin? In our condition, we know that it is virtually always our affections that rule us and lead us to sin. But that is not the only way that an opposition to the revealed will of God can arise. In an unfallen creature, it seems that it must arise in some other way. It must arise in the same way that it apparently did in Satan—by creating within the creature not a disaffection for God, not a suggestion that God is not to be loved, but a suggestion that God is too good. God is too wonderful to do what it appears he has said.

I think this is what made Satan fall. "These people—they were elect? They're going be above me? No; that doesn't make sense. That can't happen." When Satan comes to Eve, he cannot appeal to corrupt affections. Instead, he must appeal to the very thing that led to his own rebellion: intellectual autonomy. He knows that this is how a pure creature puts himself or herself into a position to disobey God. So his appeal is to disconnect Eve's reason and the fundamental convictions of her soul from the words of God's command. In connected fashion, Satan appeals to the patience, kindness, and goodness of God. He suggests a willingness in God to pass over such a small issue for the sake of an enormously good end—which is what led God to say what he said about dying. Satan whispers to Eve, "You will not surely die. I mean, you know enough of God to know that he is kind, that he is good, and that it would be against his nature to take such radical action against a creature whom he loves over something so small as eating from this tree. After all, that cannot be a moral evil—because you can eat from all these other trees, right? So why can't you eat of this tree too? It wouldn't be a moral sin. And, after all, that fruit shows us something of the character of God. Look how beautiful it is. It's pleasant to the eyes."

Satan plants a series of thoughts and questions in Eve's mind. "Look how luscious it seems to be. I wonder what it would taste like! And who knows good and evil? Who knows their very nature? Who plumbs to the bottom of them and knows absolutely more than God does? Doesn't God want you to be like him? Isn't that the purpose of all this obedience? Isn't that the purpose of his having this fellowship with you all the time? Eating it will make you wise. You will know good and evil."

Perhaps Eve, after these suggestions, thought that she *could* reason the rest of the way. She knew these good things about God. She walked with him every day. "Surely he would not kill the creatures made in his image for such a small thing as this. There must be something else involved in this. Maybe he wants us to press our thinking on this a little bit. Maybe he wants us to show how deeply we trust his goodness and to realize that he would not do something that radical to us. We will just trust his goodness. After all, if I can experience more of the creative beauty of God by taking this fruit, that would endear my soul to him forever. *Then I would be like him.* There would never be any doubt in my mind as to what is right and wrong; I would know that like God does."

So Satan wormed his way into her intellect. Without dispelling her affections, he gradually led her to assume intellectual autonomy—to consider making a choice that she thought would make her like God. Something that would please God and would give her a greater enjoyment of the beauty of the created order. So she allowed this intellectual autonomy to lead her into disobedience to a specific command of God.

But when she ate, those affections that she thought would be enlightened and exhilarated, the wisdom that she thought would show her good and evil, and the perception of the beauty of everything that God had made—*they were not enhanced at all.* They were smothered. She immediately felt that her affections were depraved, and so she made clothes for herself. She no longer had joy in her nakedness. Concupiscence had for the first time invaded her own soul.

Now, instead of having an absolute discernment of good and evil, Eve hides from God and tries to think of a way to make an excuse, not even admitting her own evil and disobedience. Everything that she had hoped she would gain she lost. But Satan, of course, had a hand in it. Satan knows how a pure heart can quickly move from its enjoyment of God into disobedience to a specific command of God, and he took that approach with Eve. And Adam played a role, too: "Why, this is my helpmeet. I've enjoyed being with her; we have joyous times with God. If she's convinced that we should do this, why

. . . the woman God gave me would not lead me astray." And so she gave to Adam, and they both ate.

They were separated from God, separated from each other, separated from themselves in their minds, and separated from nature. Everything that had given them joy, everything that had given them life—all that was now destroyed, and those affections that should have been exhilarated and elevated were now subject to the dirt of this world. Satan is the foe of God's image bearers.

In Romans 1, Paul describes what has happened now that the verdict of death has come: in the particular places where we should willingly and joyfully glory in the power and the holy beauty of the triune God, we do not glorify him as God; nor are we thankful—but we become futile in our thoughts, and our foolish hearts are darkened. Professing ourselves to be wise, we become fools (see Rom. 1:21–22). Paul is describing the whole world, but he is describing *precisely* what happened in Satan's fall and what happened in the fall of Adam and Eve.

The Foe of Christ

We see, third, that Satan is the foe of Christ:

And another sign appeared in heaven: behold, a great red dragon, with seven heads and ten horns, and on his heads seven diadems. His tail swept down a third of the stars of heaven and cast them to the earth. And the dragon stood before the woman who was about to give birth, so that when she bore her child he might devour it. She gave birth to a male child, one who is to rule all the nations with a rod of iron, but her child was caught up to God and to his throne, and the woman fled into the wilderness, where she has a place prepared by God, in which she is to be nourished for 1,260 days. . . .

And when the dragon saw that he had been thrown down to the earth, he pursued the woman who had given birth to the male child. But the woman was given the two wings of the great eagle so that she might fly from the serpent into the wilderness, to the place where she is to be nourished for a time, and times, and half a time. (Rev. 12:3–6, 13–14)

I do not make any pretensions about being an expert on Revelation, but I think there are some things that are plain in all the imagery. The woman is the church—those who have been elected before the foundation of the world. It is the existence of the church and the eternal decrees of God that then give rise to the birth of Christ, in order that the woman would be converted, saved, and protected. The great dragon is resisting this, not liking it one bit. He, the one who was cast out of heaven, now opposes everything about Christ. He wanted to kill this child, and now he will do anything he can to diminish the impact of the child. All that this child stands for—this one who is to "rule the nations with a rod of iron"—Satan hates. Satan will do everything he can to destroy this child's purposes.

Ploys of the Enemy:
Temptation in the Wilderness

We see Satan somewhat confused, or perhaps just changing tactics, in light of the progress of Jesus's life on earth. We know that he sought to kill him early, through King Herod's decree authorizing the slaughter of the newborn males in Bethlehem, and then even when Jesus was preaching in Nazareth as the people took him to a cliff to cast him over. Satan sought to make Jesus compromise at various places and in various ways, so he would not have to go to the cross—so he would not endure the humiliation of being under his Father's wrath. And just as Christ seems poised to pass through all those temptations, Satan seeks to make him wilt under the pressure of what is coming his way—the cup of suffering that he must drink.

Jesus is led by the Spirit into the wilderness "to be tempted by the devil" (Matt. 4:1). He is in an abandoned place in a weakened condition; Adam and Eve, by contrast, were in a luxurious garden in the strength of their fellowship with God. In the wilderness, Satan appeals to the intrinsic rights, power, and glory of the Son of God. "If you are the Son of God, command these stones to become loaves of bread" (v. 3). This was the kind of logic Satan used: "You have the right; you intrinsically are the Son of God. You have creative power. There's no need for you to be hungry. It is not any violation of your power or of your intrinsic glory simply to do what you've already done in creating all things—to command that these stones be made bread."

Jesus responds, "It is written, 'Man shall not live by bread alone, but by every word that comes from the mouth of God'" (v. 4). In other words, "I am like all of the creatures that I have come to save—I am dependent upon the Word of God. I am dependent upon the providence of God. I will not use my intrinsic glory or intrinsic power to create for myself a position of comfort when the very reason I am suffering this temptation is in order that I might achieve a perfect righteousness. If I intervene on my own behalf by making bread for myself, then I will not have the proper suffering and the proper dependence upon the goodness of my Father that are necessary for my righteousness. I will not live by bread alone. That is not life to me now. Life is complete submission to the Word of God."

The Word of God, which he knew very well, revealed in the covenant of redemption that he must come to suffer, must be humiliated, and must die for the sins of rebellious creatures.

"So he wants to appeal to Scripture?" Satan thinks. "I've got one myself." Psalm 91 is a messianic psalm that speaks of how God will come to the aid of his servant and in the end will display his salvation. "And there's a promise right in the middle of this psalm," Satan says. "So let's test this out: let's go up to a high place, and you jump off—because the Scripture says, 'He will command his angels concerning you,' and 'On their hands they will bear you up, lest you strike your foot against a stone' (Ps. 91:11, 12). What a great demonstration this would be of your trust in the Word of God—especially when that Word is the very place that talks about how God will show his salvation through you. This is your opportunity."

In response, Jesus quickly puts Satan's challenge in context, knowing that Psalm 91 does not say you can just test God out and jump down in order see if God is going to "snap to." This psalm was written in the context of a person who is living his life day by day with a deep trust in the providence of God—a person who makes the Word of God his food. Then, when dangers come, when all these things—in God's providence—surround us, we know that he is going to help. Jesus was convinced that, as it related to him, God the Father would bring him through all his trials. But he was not to test God's Word. He believed that God's Word was true and that, if he lived in the way the Psalm described, in the end he would indeed be shown the salvation of God. But to seek to prompt God by some extraordinary testing would be in direct violation of and disobedience to the whole spirit of the Psalm.

Now that Jesus has parried Satan's attempts to derail him by appealing to his intrinsic goodness and his position as Messiah, Satan finally seeks to get Jesus to avoid the great pain, sorrow, and suffering that are coming. Knowing his own ultimate demise, that his dominion over the kingdoms of this world will one day come to an end, Satan takes Jesus to a high hill. He brings Jesus to a place where he can see a vast expanse of the kingdom of this world. "This is what you've come for, isn't it?" Satan quips. "Right now, I'm the prince of the power of the air. Right now, I'm the one who is controlling all the sons of disobedience. I will give them over to you now, *if you just bow and worship me*—if you recognize my beauty and my intelligence. Even just for a moment, exalt me. Then you won't have to go to the cross; you won't have to suffer. You won't have to be humiliated—you can gain the victory."

Of course, Jesus knew that was not the way. Fully aware of the very purpose for which he had come, Jesus rebuked Satan again. He knew he could not gain the victory without the suffering; he knew he could not gain his people without dying for their sins. Jesus knew he would defeat Satan not by conceding to his wishes but by taking the power of death out of Satan's hand—and Jesus could do this because he himself would die that death.

Matthew's temptation account shows that Satan is the opponent of Christ, who used all his cunning and all his subtleties to insinuate himself into Jesus's thinking. The devil sought to align himself with Jesus's *apparent* purposes, hoping to gently lead him to take another way out. This is what Satan knows about how to fall away from God, and it had worked with Adam and Eve. But the new and better Adam was here, and he saw through it all and maintained the humiliation of his humanity in order to redeem his people.

Ploys of the Enemy: Anything but the Cross

We see Satan's opposition to Christ again at Caesarea Philippi. There Peter confesses the Messianic status of Jesus, and Jesus replies, "Blessed are you, Simon Bar-Jonah! For flesh and blood has not revealed this to you, but my Father who is in heaven" (Matt. 16:17). Then, as Jesus begins to tell the disciples that he will go to Jerusalem, where he will be rejected, will die, and on the third day will be raised, I don't think Peter even hears it. Peter is elated with his own status (something that Jesus had already warned the disciples against). He seems to have reasoned, *Jesus said to me, "Blessed are you." That means I'm special.*

So when Jesus begins to talk this nonsense about dying, Peter thinks, *Well, I know that he is the Christ and that he will sit on the throne of his father David. I'm putting all of this together in the right way. He will judge the nations. He will rule them with a rod of iron. If people do not kiss the Son, his anger will flare up.* And finally, Peter concludes, "So what do you mean that you're going to die? That can't happen. You shall not surely die."

Jesus recognizes the power behind Peter's words. Immediately he declares, "Get behind me, Satan! You are a hindrance to me. For you are not setting your mind on the things of God, but on the things of man" (Matt. 16:23). Peter perceived only those things that are of men—fallen men who reason their way out of obedience to God, men who love their own lives and love their own pleasures. Who love their own reason and love their own heights and positions more than they love the revealed Word of God. Peter was reasoning like men.

We also see that Jesus was conscious that Satan would come to him in those final days and would seek to convince him somehow that he was not worthy to go to the cross—that there was some way in which he had failed and could not

29

follow through. In John 14, Jesus spoke of Satan's attempt to destroy God's plan. He said to his disciples, "I will no longer talk much with you, for the ruler of this world is coming. He has no claim on me, but I do as the Father has commanded me, so that the world may know that I love the Father" (vv. 30–31).

There had never been a time when Jesus did not love the Father. There had never been a time when he did not love the Father's will for him. There had never been a time when he doubted the wisdom of the Father's way of redemption. All these things were so present in the mind of Christ—so beautiful, so illustrative of the perfections of God. Jesus loved the mission that he was on—even though from a human standpoint, and even within the framework of divine justice, the cross was something to be shunned and feared. Jesus despised the shame of the cross. Why? Because of the joy that was set before him. He endured because of the joy, and he sat down at the right hand of the throne of God (see Heb. 12:2).

Jesus loved the Father. He knew that he loved the Father with all his heart, mind, soul, and strength. He also knew that he loved his enemies and that he loved his neighbor as himself. There had never been sin in him. Jesus had received the positive command to die—the just for the unjust. That was something that was not necessarily morally obligatory but needs to be seen as a positive command, just as Adam had received the positive command not to eat of the tree in the midst of the garden—not that it was a moral problem to eat the fruit of a tree that God had made, but there was a positive command not to do it. In comparison, Jesus had a positive command that was far more difficult than Adam's—one that had all kinds of seeming contradictions in it: to lay his life down for his enemies, for those who are helpless, in obedience to his Father's command.

Yet Jesus says, "I do as the Father has commanded me." Satan had no claim on him; he could not point to anything in the consciousness of Jesus that would make Jesus doubt, for one moment, his own qualification to do what God had commanded him to do.

Ploys of the Enemy: Subverting the Message

Satan also seeks to destroy the work of Christ through the perversion of the apostolic message. Christ sent his apostles out to preach about his work: his death, resurrection, ascension, and second coming. As they preached among the nations, the world would turn and believe in Christ.

Satan wants to interrupt that plan of Christ, too. As John surveyed the reality of the last days, he wrote,

> Children, it is the last hour, and as you have heard that antichrist is coming, so now many antichrists have come. Therefore we know that it is the last hour. They went out from us, but they were not of us; for if they had been of us, they would have continued with us. But they went out, that it might become plain that they all are not of us. But you have been anointed by the Holy One, and you all have knowledge. (1 John 2:18–20)

Those who believe that Jesus is the Christ have been born of God. This is a provision of the covenant of redemption: that the Spirit would come and change our hearts and give us cause to delight in the righteousness of God's law and in the righteousness of Christ. The Spirit makes us see the beauty of the gospel as we receive it and trust in Christ alone. That is evidence of an anointing from the Holy One, and those who are so anointed will not be deceived by the antichrists who go out from them.

John later notes that "every spirit that does not confess Jesus is not from God. This is the spirit of the antichrist" (1 John 4:3). Satan is seeking to influence those who preach and, in fact, often has great success in doing so. The devil influences people who pose as preachers of the gospel to reject the apostolic message and preach a different gospel. But again John assures those who hear this: "He who is in you is greater than he who is in the world." (v. 4).

We have already seen that Satan is a perverter of God's Word in all these things. In Eden, Satan asks, "Has God indeed said?" In the wilderness, he seeks to manipulate Jesus by quoting Scripture. And now, in the church, Satan opposes the clarity of the apostolic message. John looks at the false teachers and says, "We are from God"—speaking of himself and the other apostles. "Whoever knows God listens to us; whoever is not from God does not listen to us. By this we know the Spirit of truth and the spirit of error" (v. 6). True wisdom means understanding the divine revelation, the sovereignty of God in redemption, and the obedience that is due to him as presented in his revealed Word.

Our Persistent Opponent

This leads us to another way in which Satan is our foe: he is the infiltrator of human wisdom. James is very concerned about wisdom, telling us to ask for wisdom if we lack it. But he says that we must ask in faith—that is, with a belief in the Word of God (see James 1:5–6). We must believe in the truthfulness of the Word and in the experienced application of it. We must ask in faith, without doubting, "for the one who doubts is like a wave of the sea that is driven and tossed by the wind" (v. 6). We must be not only hearers of the Word, who forget what manner of men we are after we leave the mirror, but also doers of the Word (see vv. 22–24). We must be swift to hear, slow to speak, and slow to anger (see v. 19). We must realize that God gave us birth through his Word—through the Word of truth.

When James speaks of wisdom, he says that human words that are untaught by the Word of God (i.e., the tongue) are set on fire by hell (see James 3:5–6). The tongue is a restless evil full of deadly poison (see v. 8) in that it so often mimics the premise that Satan first used: "We shall not surely die. Salvation is not that big a deal. God's wrath is not that big a deal. Sin is not that big a deal. Sin is something God can easily forgive."

This is the kind of wisdom that is from below: the tongue that is uninformed by the Word of God; human wisdom and human words that are untaught by the Spirit. James says that this kind of wisdom is earthly, unspiritual, and demonic.

Satan is also a captor who blinds the people of this world. We see in Ephesians 2 that all our affections—all those mentalities and gifts that God has given us—are now perverted in such a way that they serve sin and Satan. The passions of our flesh, Paul says, were captive to these. It is "the prince of the power of the air, the spirit that is now at work in the sons of disobedience" who takes advantage of all those things that are characteristic of our own internal natures (v. 2). Now we are directly in Satan's path. We reason like Satan. We are pliable for him. Our affections are what he wants them to be. We place ultimate value and sensate pleasure in the wrong things and not in those things that are eternal. Our inward, curved rationality is now used to serve our own pleasures—to serve the things of this world—and we use them to turn away from God. Our nature is so corrupted and devilish that it is the very object of wrath itself. We are by nature children of wrath, Paul declares (see v. 3).

Free Grace for Us

Satan's temptations have indeed made a moral wreck of the divine image. And were it not for divine sovereignty, for the revelation that we have in the covenant of redemption, for the fact that God's sheep will not follow the thief and that our names are written in heaven—were it not for those realities that are clearly revealed throughout Scripture, we might very well despair and say, "Yes, Satan has won." Our wills and our affections and our pleasures dominate us in a godless way, and we are by nature children deserving of wrath. This is not just a misfortune; it is a moral tragedy. Yet, in that very same passage, Paul exalts the freeness of the grace of God:

> But God, being rich in mercy, because of the great love with which he loved us, even when we were dead in our trespasses, made us alive together with Christ—by grace you have been saved—and raised us up with him and seated us with him in the heavenly places in Christ Jesus, so that in the coming ages he might show the immeasurable riches of his grace in kindness toward us in Christ Jesus. For by grace you have been saved through faith. And this is not your own doing; it is the gift of God, not a result of works, so that no one may boast. (Eph. 2:4–9)

We move from the ruin that Satan has brought upon us into rejoicing in the sovereign grace of God, as the Scriptures clearly reveal. "Do not rejoice in this, that the spirits are subject to you, but rejoice that your names are written in heaven"

(Luke 10:20). "The god of this world has blinded the minds of the unbelievers, to keep them from seeing the light of the gospel of the glory of Christ" (2 Cor. 4:4). My, what blindness. They can't see light? They can't see the light of the glory of God and the face of Christ? How blind! And yet the God who said, "Let light shine out of darkness," has shone in our hearts, giving us that very knowledge. God has illuminated our hearts with the glory and beauty of Christ the Savior, showing us the wondrous mercy of God the Father. We have the Spirit of God, who has come to dwell within us—even while we still have indwelling sin—to sanctify us, to make us cry, "Abba, Father!"

Satan has failed miserably. He plunged the image bearers into sin, but through it the matchless grace and power of God have been magnified. Yet Satan remains the foe of Christ redeemed. For "it was allowed to make war on the saints and to conquer them. And authority was given it over every tribe and people and language and nation, and all who dwell on earth will worship it, everyone whose name has not been written before the foundation of the world in the book of life of the Lamb who was slain" (Rev. 13:7–8). Job was the subject of heavenly discussion, and Satan was allowed to test him (see Job 1). David was incited to take a census, showing that Satan himself can be one who is used to execute God's justice (see 1 Chron. 21:1). As Paul says,

> For we do not wrestle against flesh and blood, but against the rulers, against the authorities, against the cosmic powers over this present darkness, against the spiritual forces of evil in the heavenly places. Therefore take up the whole armor of God, that you may be able to withstand in the evil day, and having done all, to stand firm. (Eph. 6:12–13)

Or, as Peter reminds us,

Be sober-minded; be watchful. Your adversary the devil prowls around like a roaring lion, seeking someone to devour. Resist him, firm in your faith, knowing that the same kinds of suffering are being experienced by your brotherhood throughout the world. And after you have suffered a little while, the God of all grace, who has called you to his eternal glory in Christ, will himself restore, confirm, strengthen, and establish you. To him be the dominion forever and ever. Amen. (1 Peter 5:8–11)

Satan's dominion is not forever. His attempts to destroy us are merely tools in the divine purpose, to perfect us according to the call of God's grace and Christ Jesus. "That ancient serpent"—the devil, also known as Satan, the deceiver of the whole world—will be felled with "one little word." What is that word? Martin Luther knew the answer:

> That word above all earthly powers,
> No thanks to them, abideth;
> The Spirit and the gifts are ours
> Through Him who with us sideth:
> Let goods and kindred go,
> This mortal life also;
> The body they may kill:
> *God's truth abideth still,*
> His Kingdom is forever.[3]

May God allow us to see the richness of his grace and mercy. May God give us grace to know his Word, to read his Word, to believe his Word, and to understand his Word in

---

3. Martin Luther, "A Mighty Fortress Is Our God," 1529; trans. Frederic H. Hedge, 1853.

every way we can—but never to violate its propositions or violate its truth. May God establish us and sanctify us by his truth, and may we always subject our rationality and our affections to those simple, powerful words: "Thus saith the Lord."

3

Malevolent Methodology

RONALD L. KOHL

Ephesians 4:26–27

IF NOTHING ELSE, when it comes to the work of the enemy of our souls, the Bible screams out a persistent message to us: "You've been warned!" Whether or not we heed the warnings is, sadly, another story.

As a Civil War veteran, Captain William Fetterman should have known better when a small group of Sioux, Cheyenne, and Arapaho enticed him to take his small troop of eighty men away from the safety of Fort Phil Kearny, in Wyoming, in hot pursuit across the tall prairie grasses of the Powder River country. Enticing soldiers with a small decoy party was a common Native American tactic that had worked many times before. Fetterman was aware of it. But he ignored the warnings and rode, along with his men, into an ambush. Probably the only reason his name is unfamiliar to most of us is because ten years later, in 1876, George Armstrong Custer largely repeated

Fetterman's mistake of underestimating the foe at the Little Bighorn. We all know what happened to him, don't we? Fetterman's mistake wasn't ignorance; it was arrogance. His enemy used familiar methods, but Fetterman failed to take either his enemy or his enemy's tactics seriously; and, in less than half an hour after being surrounded by a thousand warriors, an officer who had earlier boasted that "with eighty men, I could ride through the whole Sioux Nation" was dead—along with a party of exactly eighty troopers.[1]

We ignore warnings at our peril. And that suits Satan just fine. The enemy of our souls wants us to ignore not only his means, but the reality of his very existence. We wouldn't do that, would we? We understand that a historical-literal hermeneutic of Scripture requires that we believe in the reality of Satan. But all too often, I fear that we live as if we believe Satan is, for the most part, an absentee landlord who only rarely checks in on his tenants. Or a lazy warrior who devotes his energies to staying in camp rather than planning attacks on Christian believers.

C. S. Lewis hit on that very concept in his classic work *The Screwtape Letters*. "There are two equal and opposite errors into which our race can fall about the Devils," Lewis wrote. "One is to disbelieve in their existence. The other is to believe, and to feel an excessive and unhealthy interest in them. They themselves are equally pleased by both errors and hail a materialist or a magician with the same delight."[2]

1. Stephen E. Ambrose wrote of Fetterman, "Like his opposite number, Crazy Horse [who was part of the party that annihilated Fetterman's unit], Fetterman was itching for a fight; unlike Crazy Horse, Fetterman knew next to nothing of his enemy. That simple fact gave Crazy Horse an enormous advantage." Stephen E. Ambrose, *Crazy Horse and Custer: The Parallel Lives of Two American Warriors* (Garden City, NY: Doubleday, 1975), 232. Ambrose deals with the Fetterman Massacre in considerable detail on pages 231–43.
2. C. S. Lewis, *The Screwtape Letters* (New York: Macmillan, 1976), 3.

40

"Sometimes leaders appear too embarrassed to speak of the Devil and evil spirits," Thabiti Anyabwile notes. "We hear the devotees of scientism telling us that we are backwards and unenlightened. But the light of God's Word shines squarely on Satan, the accuser of the brothers, as the source of this evil. We serve no one by pretending that Satan does not exist. He does. And he wreaks havoc on those blinded to his devices."[3]

Are there those who find themselves absolutely absorbed with the devil's work in our world and lives? Absolutely. But I think they are greatly outnumbered by those who fall prey to the Fetterman debacle: they disregard the general principle of spiritual warfare and thus find themselves easy pickings when our adversary finds a foothold and exploits it. *Foothold*. It's a fitting word where Satan is concerned. It's an entirely biblical word, too. Ephesians 4:27 says, "Give no opportunity to the devil." The word translated "opportunity" in Greek is *topon*—"place." And a foothold is the very definition of a place—"a place where a person may stand or walk securely; a secure position, especially a firm basis for further progress or development."[4]

In Ephesians 4, Paul is speaking about ungodly anger. When we give way to allowing the fuse of anger to be lit and then explode, we provide a place for the devil to operate in our lives. And once we give him an inch, he takes a mile. He's like the ultimate overstaying-his-welcome dinner guest. Benjamin Franklin once said, "Fish and visitors smell after three days." That's the rough idea. We give Satan a foothold, and that's all he needs to hang around and torment us for years.

The devil is glad to exploit anger as a chink in our spiritual armor—but he'll use most anything, really. Lust. Idolatry.

3. Thabiti M. Anyabwile, *Finding Faithful Elders and Deacons* (Wheaton, IL: Crossway, 2012), 114.

4. Dictionary.com, s.v. "foothold," accessed December 6, 2018, https://www.dictionary.com/browse/foothold.

There are any number of areas that Satan delights to use in order to wedge his way into our lives, and before long— *voila!*—we've become engaged in habitual sin. We've become easy pickings. But we didn't have to be. Recognizing Satan's tactics could have helped us to steer clear and to apply the spiritual armor that God has provided for us. What are the devil's methods? They are many, and they are subtle; but I'd like to highlight four of them.

I want to focus on lies, deception, temptation, and accusation, because the Bible clearly attributes each of these methods to our adversary. They are not entirely independent entities; they often work in tandem, by the devil's design. Satan tempts us by lying. He deceives us by promising falsehoods, but the lies that he tells are enticing. They tempt us. And, of course, the devil works both sides of the street. He tempts us with lurid promises of enjoyment and satisfaction, and once we fall, he accuses us. So his methods work like a spider's web, with each strand linked to the others. And we need to mirror Paul, who in 2 Corinthians 2:10–11 wrote,

> Anyone whom you forgive, I also forgive. Indeed, what I have forgiven, if I have forgiven anything, has been for your sake in the presence of Christ, so that we would not be outwitted by Satan; for we are not ignorant of his designs.

Lies, Lies, and More Lies

"You will not surely die," the serpent said to Eve. "For God knows that when you eat of it your eyes will be opened, and you will be like God, knowing good and evil." There, in Genesis 3:4–5, Satan revealed one of his favorite methods. As usual, he couched it in truths and half-truths. That's the thing about a good liar—the lie has to sound plausible, and he often heightens this plausibility by sprinkling in some truth. Maybe even mostly truth.

Yes, the eyes of Eve and Adam were opened. Yes, they had a new understanding of good and evil. Evil might not have even been theoretical to them before; now it would be experiential. So in that respect, the serpent spoke truth. But death entered our first parents' world that day—that day when Satan lied to them and revealed himself as an eager speaker of falsehoods.

In John 8, as Jesus was engaged in a prolonged discussion with a group of Jews who included some Pharisees, the conversation turned to the subject of paternity. Jesus had done the unthinkable—he had referred to God not only as "the Father" but as "my Father." Some heard Jesus's words and believed, but the Pharisees dealt with the paternity question by declaring, "Abraham is our father," to which Jesus countered, "*If* you were Abraham's children, you would be doing the works Abraham did, but now you seek to kill me, a man who has told you the truth that I heard from God. This is not what Abraham did" (vv. 39–40).

If the point were not already clear, Jesus's next statement drove it home: "You are doing what your father did" (v. 41). He accused them of being the offspring of those who had consistently opposed God and God's messengers, the prophets. And then, moments later, he identified their spiritual father:

> If God were your Father, you would love me, for I came from God and I am here. I came not of my own accord, but he sent me. Why do you not understand what I say? It is because you cannot bear to hear my word. You are of your father the devil, and your will is to do your father's desires. He was a murderer from the beginning, and does not stand in the truth, because there is no truth in him. When he lies,

he speaks out of his own character, for he is a liar and the
father of lies. (vv. 42–44)

The Pharisees, he said, were spiritual progeny of the devil,
as proved by their reaction to and treatment of Jesus. They were
bearing the marks of their father. Like father, like son? Yes,
that was true and would be proven even more truthful in time,
when the Pharisees would play a key role in nailing Jesus to the
cross. But they were already bearing the family characteristics
of their father, the devil, who is both a liar and a murderer.

Satan as murderer—to what could Jesus have been referring? Could he have been alluding to Cain and Abel? Genesis
4 records the first post-fall crime, as Cain slew his brother.
Satan was clearly an accomplice to that first murder. But no,
we must go two chapters earlier—to the fall itself. For Satan
had told Eve, "You will not surely die." A lie? Yes, but also murder, as John MacArthur notes: "Satan's temptation of Adam
and Eve brought about their spiritual death and that of the
entire human race."[5] Eve did not die that day, but on that day
death entered the world. *Murder* became part of the human
vocabulary.

When Jesus said to the Pharisees, "You are of your father
the devil. . . . When he lies, he speaks out of his own character,
for he is a liar and the father of lies," he was noting that the
Pharisees' propensity for falsehood identified their true paternity. They were showing their true stripes, and in "outing"
them, Jesus was speaking some powerful truths about Satan.
First, he was absolutely declaring the devil's existence—not as
some nebulous concept, but as a person who must be taken
seriously. And second, our Lord was identifying one of Satan's

5. John MacArthur, *The MacArthur New Testament Commentary: John
1–11* (Chicago: Moody Publishers, 2006), 372.

44

methods: he loves to lie, and always for the purpose of contributing to his targets' spiritual harm.

How is Satan an effective liar? He is successful in that neither his lies nor the liar himself are easily identifiable. Subtlety is one of his hallmarks. The Pharisees were generally considered to be the protectors of the law—people to be supported and respected. It took an expert—Jesus in his omniscience—to recognize that malevolence lay beneath the Pharisees' veneer of religion and adherence to Torah and Mishnah.

We are not omniscient. But we have not been left without weapons. God gives us his Word, and he gives us increasing discernment and wisdom through the means of grace that he has made available to us, so that we begin to increasingly recognize Satan's work. He calls us to Berean mind-sets, so that we search and know the Scriptures. As we do, we find ourselves increasingly able to see the latest lie that our enemy is peddling.

Two childhood games come to mind as reminders of the necessity of recognizing Satan's lie: hide-and-seek and peek-a-boo. In hide-and-seek, a line must be drawn between seeking and finding. I'm reminded of one of my favorite scenes from the 1981 film *Arthur*. When the adorable drunken millionaire Arthur Bach (where else will you ever see those three words joined together?), played by Dudley Moore, relates to his valet Hobson (Sir John Gielgud) the fondness of his memories of playing hide-and-seek when he was a child, he asks Hobson whether he remembers when "I used to hide, and you never found me." Hobson replies, "Did you know I never looked?"[6]

Diligence in recognizing Satan's presence and lies comes through vigilance. May we never be those who fall prey to the lies of the chief of liars because we are not looking for them and

6. "Caring for Hobson," *Arthur*, directed by Steve Gordon (1981; Burbank, CA: Warner Home Video, 1997), DVD.

so don't recognize them when the world, the flesh, and the devil come tempting us with what sounds both plausible and desirable. Paul's advice in Romans 16:19, as he warns the Christians in Rome to be watchful for false teachers, is particularly applicable: "I want you to be wise as to what is good and innocent as to what is evil." The J.B. Phillips paraphrase reads, "I want to see you experts in good, and not even beginners in evil."

That doesn't mean that we adopt an "ignorance is bliss" posture. Perhaps Paul was thinking of Jesus's own words when he wrote Romans 16:19, for in Matthew 10, Jesus knew he was sending the apostles out to engage in ministry in a hostile environment. "Behold, I am sending you out as sheep in the midst of wolves, so be wise as serpents and innocent as doves" (v. 16). Paul is urging the Roman believers to love good so much that they recognize it and run to it as experts in pursuing what is good. But as far as evil, they should know just enough about it that they quickly identify it and flee from it. Where do we learn what good is? Where do we identify truth? There is no magic or secret. We need to be well-versed in the Scripture, immersed in the Bible. Satan's subtle lies are exposed for what they are the same way that the US Secret Service identifies counterfeit bills: by lining them up against the truth.

That brings me to peek-a-boo—an utterly simple game played with infants. You peek, you boo, and then you declare, "I see you!" We need to do that more frequently with our adversary. We need to call out, "I see you! I know what you're doing! I recognize your hand at work!" Taking that approach won't change or deter our enemy, but it's for our benefit. It helps us to more quickly and easily understand that we are engaged in spiritual warfare against an enemy who "doth seek to work us woe" and is "armed with cruel hate." Satan is a dangerous foe, but he is not omniscient. He is uncanny in honing in on our weaknesses. He can easily recognize an open door or an undefended flank. But he doesn't know everything. And that means that a verbal rebuke, in the name of Jesus, is an effective defense. James's advice in James 4:7 is for our benefit: "Resist the devil, and he will flee from you."

Deceiver Extraordinaire

Some disguises are laughable; there's no other way to describe them. I grew up in an era of fake eyeglasses and mustaches. Trust me—no one was fooled by a 29-cent disguise. But the devil is no joke as a deceiver. He is the deceiver extraordinaire, misleading with word, deed, motive, and even appearance. The Bible frequently portrays Satan in this light—as one who portrays himself to be what he is not. And he is effective in that role and will remain effective until near the end, as portrayed by John in Revelation 12:9. "And the great dragon was thrown down, that ancient serpent, who is called the devil and Satan, the deceiver of the whole world—he was thrown down to the earth, and his angels were thrown down with him."

"The deceiver of the whole world." That's no small (dis) honor. By this John does not mean that every single person is deceived, for the elect will not be led astray. But he successfully blinds the minds of unbelievers; it is no stretch to suggest, as John Piper notes, that all unbelievers are "sons [and daughters] of the devil."[7] It is no wonder that Vern Poythress can say, "Satan uses deceit as his main weapon."[8]

7. John Piper, "The Truth Will Set You Free" (sermon, Bethlehem Baptist Church, Minneapolis, MN, March 19, 2011), available online at https://www.desiringgod.org/messages/the-truth-will-set-you-free. The full quote reads as follows: "Jesus spoke of all unbelievers, Jews and Gentiles, not just Jews, as sons of the devil."

8. Vern S. Poythress, *The Returning King: A Guide to the Book of Revelation*

In 2 Corinthians 11, Paul offers a strident warning against those who serve as Satan's instruments and who follow their master's lead in deception. They present a false gospel that is particularly dangerous, because the easily deceived fall prey to accepting it as the true gospel. Paul rightly traced their errors back to their source in verse 3: "I am afraid that as the serpent deceived Eve by his cunning, your thoughts will be led astray from a sincere and pure devotion to Christ." The concept: Satan deceived Eve.[9] In the same way, false teachers will deceive you if you don't exercise discernment. And that's no small thing, Paul notes, for Satan "disguises himself as an angel of light. So it is no surprise if his servants, also, disguise themselves as servants of righteousness" (vv. 14–15).

How, you might ask, can someone as purely evil as Satan disguise himself as an angel of light? How can anyone be so foolish as to be deceived by the devil? It's easier than we think—especially when we consider that his vast array of powers includes the ability to produce "false signs and wonders" (2 Thess. 2:9). Satan's primary means of deception makes use of our minds. If the devil can turn our thinking aside, even a little bit, from the straight path of following the truth as God has revealed it in Scripture, he can move our wills in any number of different ways. In *The Screwtape Letters,* C. S. Lewis highlights how this type of deception comes into play in areas such as our commitment to fully follow Jesus Christ in all-of-life obedience. Listen to this interchange between the senior demon Screwtape and his fledgling nephew Wormwood as an example of how Satan trumpets moderation in matters

(Phillipsburg, NJ: P&R Publishing, 2000), 143–44.

9. Paul tells us in 1 Timothy 2:14 that Adam was not deceived, but his obvious presence in the garden while the serpent came calling doesn't say much for his commitment to God's clear instruction concerning the tree of the knowledge of good and evil.

of faith: "If you can once get him to the point of thinking that 'religion is all very well up to a point,' you can feel quite happy about his soul. A moderated religion is as good for us as no religion at all—and more amusing."[10]

Satan deceives by making falsehood attractive and by promising a payoff that he cannot deliver. And that brings us to his next favorite ploy: temptation.

The Tempter . . . Always at Work

Of all the names or titles attached to Satan, the title *tempter* is the one that perhaps best suits him, for it is a title given to him in Scripture and it accurately describes his methods. "For this reason," Paul writes in 1 Thessalonians 3:5, "when I could bear it no longer, I sent to learn about your faith, for fear that somehow the tempter had tempted you and our labor would be in vain." When Jesus instructs us to pray, "And lead us not into temptation, but deliver us from evil" (Matt. 6:13), he is addressing the reality of Satan's tempting power. There would be no need to pray for rescue if the devil's temptations were easily thwarted. We all know that isn't the case. Satan pairs desirable bait with an enticing sales pitch, and so our vigilance must be constant. See if any of these approaches sound familiar:

Taste just a bit of this. I promise you'll really like it. One of the devil's most proven types of bait is the bait of pleasure. And sin is pleasurable—at least for a season. Or a moment. See the danger inherent in this approach. If broccoli-eating were a sin, Satan could tempt us all day long, but to no avail. (Unless, of course, you're gaga about broccoli. Then you've got other

10. Lewis, *The Screwtape Letters*, 43.

problems.) But no—the devil tempts us with sinful pleasures that are actually pleasurable. The bait is hard to resist.

Indulge yourself. You deserve some enjoyment. Our adversary often combines temptation with flattery. If the devil can disguise himself as an angel of light, he is just as able to tempt us by appearing to be a friend even though he's our sworn enemy. He appeals to our pride and our sense of entitlement, and in so doing, he proves that Proverbs 16:18 is deadly accurate: "Pride goes before destruction, and a haughty spirit before a fall."

Don't worry. You're in control. You can stop anytime you like. Satan trivializes temptation, making it seem like a game we can play without penalty and can win in our own strength. Turning again to Proverbs, we see wisdom saying, "Can a man carry fire next to his chest and his clothes not be burned?" (Prov. 6:27). Visualize that. The answer is clearly no—and yet we think we can play with sin and escape unscathed. No one dabbles in sin, really. Once we engage, we're ensnared.

Rationalize your behavior. This is one of Satan's choicest methods—to encourage us into self-excusing sinful behavior. If we explode at a fellow motorist, indulging our predilection toward angry outbursts, the ploy that he whispers in our ear might sound like, "The target of your behavior had it coming." If the temptation is to a private sin, he may employ another tactic: "This hurts nobody. And it doesn't harm you, either." That, of course, is not true. It's a foothold that Satan will employ again and again—and often with increasing payoff as we slide further and further into sinful habits.

If the tempter's means are so successful, and so multifaceted, what hope is there for us? Well, there is prayer—and the

50

importance and value of prayer must never be trivialized. As Jesus came to the garden of Gethsemane, he urged his disciples, "Pray that you may not enter into temptation." Certainly, with the cross just hours away, our Lord was focusing on a particular trial, but the principle applies to all believers in all circumstances. Prayer is a powerful tool that has been supplied for our use, and one of the benefits that we have, as we pray, is the knowledge that the object of our prayers understands us. He knows what it means to be tempted, for he was himself tempted by the devil. And so he offers this hope to us as we cry out to him:

> Since then we have a great high priest who has passed through the heavens, Jesus, the Son of God, let us hold fast our confession. For we do not have a high priest who is unable to sympathize with our weaknesses, but one who in every respect has been tempted as we are, yet without sin. Let us then with confidence draw near to the throne of grace, that we may receive mercy and find grace to help in time of need. (Heb. 4:14–16)

From Temptation to Accusation

When Satan's temptations lead us to succumb, then what? You know the answer: shame. And accusation. Satan has earned another of his titles: the accuser of the brethren (see Rev. 12:10). Accusation is one of his particular delights, as we see in the early chapters of Job. The title character of that book is introduced as "blameless and upright." Job wasn't without sin, but he was sensitive to it in all areas—not only in his own life, but also in the lives of his children. Job 1:5 tells us that he would present early-morning burnt offerings on their behalf—not because he was sure they had engaged in sin, but on the possibility that they had done so. "It may be that my children have sinned, and cursed God in their hearts." This was Job's "continual" practice—reminding us that (1) he was one of the least likely candidates for Satan to accuse, and (2) that didn't matter. Our adversary accuses every Christian believer—or at least tries to.

Satan makes his entrance by coming into God's presence. He clearly has an agenda. And so when God pleads Job's case—"Have you considered my servant Job, that there is none like him on the earth, a blameless and upright man, who fears God and turns away from evil?" (v. 8)—Satan cannot wait to accuse:

> Does Job fear God for no reason? Have you not put a hedge around him and his house and all that he has, on every side? You have blessed the work of his hands, and his possessions have increased in the land. But stretch out your hand and touch all that he has, and he will curse you to your face. (vv. 9–11)

In Job's case, accusation came before there was any merit for it. Indeed, Satan accused Job not of sinning, not of falling to temptation, not of buying in to one of Satan's lies, but because he felt that Job was sheltered to the point where Satan didn't have adequate opportunity to roll out his full arsenal against him. And we are reminded that accusation sometimes comes independent of any particular failure on our part. It just comes because Satan is our accuser and will do anything to bring harm to our lives and testimonies as followers of the Lord Jesus. He is the enemy of our souls, remember? But Job doesn't recognize his presence. Job doesn't even consider the possibility that Satan is in the background, wielding power and causing Job great peril by God's permissive will. He is like so many of us in that regard: oblivious to the reality of spiritual warfare because we cannot actually see our adversary.

Job's moral compass so consistently pointed due north that God referred to Job as "my servant." The sad truth, however, is that most of us cannot say we are as upright as Job in terms of our behavior. We do fall prey to Satan's temptations. We do listen to his lies. We are more easily deceived than we like to admit. We must say, along with the apostle John in 1 John 1:10, "If we say that we have no sin, we deceive ourselves, and the truth is not in us" (KJV). And Satan works that side of the street, too. He deftly switches from tempter to accuser. His approach as tempter: "Everyone does it. There's no harm in doing it. Why not just go ahead and do it?" His approach as accuser: "How could you *do* such a thing—you who profess Jesus Christ? So much for your faith—and for the object of your faith, too, for that matter."

At this point, what are we to do? Waver in our assurance? Collapse in defeat? Satan would have us respond in that way, for a defeated Christian is a silent Christian, a somber Christian, and a sidelined Christian when it comes to active ministry for our Lord's glory. And the road is littered with genuine believers who have failed to recognize the devil's methods and have thus ridden into satanic ambush. The good news: God has given us remedies that are more proven and dependable than Satan's methods of attack.

I have been preaching through Romans. After three and a half years in this marvelous epistle, we are nearing its close. It struck me, as I began to study Romans 16, that the first direct mention of Satan in the letter doesn't appear until Romans 16:20, when Paul writes, "The God of peace will soon crush Satan under your feet." Paul has devoted almost sixteen full chapters to the glorious gospel of salvation in Christ alone, by grace alone, through faith alone, for the glory of God alone; and only at the end, in his concluding remarks, does the apostle finally reference the enemy of the gospel by name—and then only to remind his readers in Rome that Satan's days are numbered and that he will be crushed in the fulfillment of the promise made in the garden of Eden back in Genesis 3:15, as God addressed the serpent thusly: "I will put enmity between you and the woman, and between your offspring and her offspring; he shall bruise [crush] your head, and you shall bruise his heel."

In Romans 16:20, we see the word *soon*: "The God of peace will *soon* crush Satan under your feet." It's tempting to question the validity of Paul's statement. "Soon, Paul? You wrote Romans about thirty years after Christ's earthly ministry. Now we're well into the twenty-first century. I'm not sure I like your definition of *soon*." Paul's answer is that we are not to think in terms of time chronology but in terms of redemptive history. Christ has come? Check. He has died an atoning death? Check. He was buried but was raised from the dead? Check. He has ascended into glory and now is at the Father's right hand, where he makes intercession on behalf of the redeemed whenever Satan brings his accusations against them? Finally, and thankfully, check! With these truths ringing in our ears, we must remember that the only remaining event in the story of redemption is Christ's return and Satan's final defeat.

Do we still deal with sin? Do we still sometimes fail to recognize the devil's attacks and underestimate the potency of the adversary's tactics? Certainly. The war is won, but there are yet battles and skirmishes to be fought—always with the understanding that Jesus is Christus Victor and that the struggle between God and Satan is so unequal as to be laughable. The devil is a defeated foe, though he is stubbornly slow to capitulate. And so we go to war—but with God's promises going before us as an encouraging banner: "My little children, I am writing these things to you so that you may not sin. But if anyone does sin, we have an advocate with the Father, Jesus Christ the righteous" (1 John 2:1).

In *Pilgrim's Progress*, it was those promises that strengthened Christian against every attack of the enemy. As he was led on a tour of the Armory by Charity and Prudence, two of the four mistresses of the Palace Beautiful, John Bunyan supplied his readers with these delightful words: "The next day they took him, and had him into the Armory, where they shewed him all manner of Furniture, which their Lord had provided for Pilgrims, as Sword, Shield, Helmet, Breast-plate, All-Prayer, and Shoes that would not wear out. And there was here enough of this to harness out as many men, for service of their Lord, as there be Stars in the Heaven for multitude."[11]

May that be our comfort, our hope, and our strength as we recognize the devil's methods and do battle against him, clothed in the Lord's mighty armor.

---

11. John Bunyan, *The Pilgrim's Progress* (repr., Edinburgh, UK: Banner of Truth Trust, 2017), 57.

4

The World, the Flesh, and the Devil

DEREK W. H. THOMAS

Colossians 3:1–11

THERE ARE two aspects of sanctification: mortification, which is negative, and vivification, which is positive. Paul begins to describe vivification in Colossians 3:12, saying, "Put on then, as God's chosen ones, holy and beloved," and then he proceeds to list the characteristics of the holy, sanctified life. But my task in this chapter is to write about the negative aspect of putting to death and putting off. "For if you live according to the flesh you will die, but if by the Spirit you put to death the deeds of the body, you will live" (Rom. 8:13).[1]

---

1. The Greek words for *put to death* in Colossians 3:5 and Romans 8:13 are synonyms, which both mean "to put to death, to mortify"—in both cases referring to the mortification of sin.

As Christians, how can we develop a mastery over self, on the one hand, and grow in our ability to overcome sin and temptation on the other? In short, we must take the reality of ongoing sin seriously. To do this, we can explore what the New Testament has to say about mortification in terms of its *mind-set*, *motives*, and *method* (we're talking about mortification, so I chose three Ms).

The Mind-set

When it comes to our mind-set, we must first realize that we *need* to deal with sin. That's the mind-set of a Christian. Here in Colossians 3, Paul is giving us something of the "ABCs of the Christian life," outlining the structure and parameters of how to define life as a Christian. There was an old self—an Adamic self; but now that we are in Christ, we are a new self (see vv. 9–10). We have a new identity—a new humanity. As Paul writes in 2 Corinthians 5:17, "Therefore, if anyone is in Christ, he is a new creation. The old has passed away; behold, the new has come."

Paul introduces his letter to the Colossians this way: "To the saints and faithful brothers in Christ at Colossae" (1:2). We are saints—brothers in Christ. With Christ as our elder brother, we are the children of the living God. We are the holy ones; we don't have to struggle for two hundred years through purgatory in order to become saints. If you believe in Jesus, you are a saint. God reckons you to be holy and set apart in Christ.

What does that mean? According to Romans 6, it means that "sin will have no dominion over you" (v. 14). Sin is no longer your master. You may think that it's your master. You may live as if it's your master. But it is no longer your master. Consider that wonderful story about Martin Luther, who said he could at times hear the devil knocking on the door and asking, "Is Martin Luther here?" And Luther would reply, "Martin Luther doesn't live here anymore! A man in Christ lives here now!"

You can throw your ink pots at the devil and tell him that sin no longer has dominion over you. Sin is no longer your master, your ruler, your dictator. But the fact of the matter is that we sin every day. We are saints in Christ—new creations; yet we still sin. And we need to deal with that. As John Owen used to say, "Be killing sin, or it will be killing you." We need to have the mind-set that we are at war. The world, the flesh, and the devil are defeated enemies, but they are still enemies nevertheless.

That's one part of our mind-set—that we must deal with sin. But we must also realize that *we are able to deal with sin.* Before we were in Christ, we had no ground to stand against sin. Sin said "Jump," and we asked, "How high?" But now, because we are in union with Christ, we are able to deal with sin. We have died with Christ. We have been buried with Christ. We have been raised with Christ. We sit in heavenly places with Christ Jesus. The great body blow to sin has already been dealt.

We *died* to sin. What does Paul mean by this? Is he talking about the point at which we came to faith—when we were regenerated by the indwelling Holy Spirit? Perhaps; but I think Paul means more than that—he means to take us all the way back to the cross. Every single person on the planet is in union either with Adam or with Christ. One of the great truths about us as Christians is that we are now in union with Christ and are no longer under Adam, and this means that we have power over sin. We are indwelt by the Holy Spirit. We have the resources, new affections, new desires, and a will that comports to the will of God.

Everything about us is different—and not just spiritually but physically. I remember attending the funeral of a man—a godly man and an elder in the church who had six sons. Three of the sons were Christians, and three of them were not. As I looked at the six of them in the room, I noticed that the Christians spoke and looked differently from their non-Christian brothers. You could see the effect of the gospel on three of them and the total lack of effect of it on the others.

Those sons were all brought up in the same home, hearing the same things and having the same opportunities. Yet Christ's union with three of them changed them in a tangible way, shaping their attitudes and demeanor. That's the power we have in Christ. We need to deal with sin—but we also have the ability to deal with sin, through the spiritual resources that come with being in Christ.

We need to deal with sin, and we are able to deal with sin. Now let me suggest a third conviction: we must *want* to deal with sin. Ah—there's the issue. Do you really want to deal with sin? I'm talking about sins in your own life. I'm talking about sins that have become like your pets—like your dog or your cat or whatever pet you have. The thing with pets is that you love to spoil them. My dog is absolutely ruined. He sleeps on our bed. He's eighty pounds, and he would push us out of bed if he could. I've spent a fortune on training him, and it was a waste of money. When people come to the house and we are perhaps giving them some coffee and maybe a cookie or two, the dog is right there underneath them, slobbering, drooling. We say, "Excuse the dog," and so on.

We treat our sins like that. We spoil them, and we excuse them. But the question of mind-set remains: do you *want* to deal with sin? Because if you don't, you might as well stop reading now. If you want compromise, you'll get it in large doses. Maybe that's the issue—that you're content with a certain kind of Christian life that isn't extreme. That's the problem with our society: anyone who is extreme about something is labeled a "fundamentalist" or a "radical." We're terrified of radical Islam, aren't we? Even, perhaps, of radical Christianity?

We want the world to love us and like us, and so we want to become like the world—excusing our sins and refusing to face them. Do you desire to deal with sin? Do you want to kill sin? Do you want to get rid of it? Do you want it out of your life?

The Motives

From mind-set we move on to motives, and I want to talk about three of them. First, you reap what you sow (see Gal. 6:7). Consider Colossians 3:5–6:

> Put to death therefore what is earthly in you: sexual immorality, impurity, passion, evil desire, and covetousness, which is idolatry. On account of these the wrath of God is coming.

What's the motivation for Christian living? There are people today who say that the only motivation is gratitude. Gratitude is indeed a basic motivation. Get that wrong, and you're into legalism. Get that wrong, and you get the grammar of the gospel wrong. The imperatives must always be based on the indicatives. And yet gratitude is not the only motive, for we see another one right here in verse 6: "the wrath of God is coming." Why do you need to deal with sin? Because if you don't, the wrath of God is coming. We're talking about the reflex of God's holiness against sin.

You say, "But I'm a forgiven man" or "I'm a forgiven woman. My sins have all been blotted out." Well, that's true, my friend—if you're a Christian. But how do you know that you're a Christian? How do you know that you're in Christ? Part of the answer to that question is your ongoing sanctification. Is there fruit? In Matthew 7:20, Jesus declared the difference between those with true faith and those who only profess faith in Christ. "Thus you will recognize them by their fruits." You say that you believe in Jesus, but what's the evidence that you believe in Jesus? Is there enough evidence to convict you if you were brought before a court of law and charged with being a Christian? Because, if you don't engage in a lifelong battle with sin, there may be insufficient evidence. It may be that you're just kidding yourself. It may be that you're a hypocrite—that you have just some nominal Christianity and have been caught, as it were, in the flow of things. Is there evidence?

"You reap what you sow." We tend to think of things in short-term ways. Put a small coin before your eyes and it will blot out a check for a million dollars that is made out in your name. You can't see the check, because all you can see is the small coin before your eyes. You say, "Well, I'll have this coin," never perceiving the true treasure that's right in front of you.

There's an old saying that goes, "Sow a thought and reap an act. Sow an act and reap a character. Sow a character and reap a destiny." So what will be your ultimate harvest? If you don't deal with ongoing sin—if you just leave it alone, if you treat it as a pet, if you feed it and maybe you give it a secret little room in your house, when no one is at home, and you think, *Well, I can do this and no one will know*—God does know. Paul is saying that "on account of these, the wrath of God is coming."

This isn't Derek Thomas saying this; this is Paul, speaking to Christians. He is speaking to those who are in Christ—who are a new self, a new humanity—and he's saying, "If you don't engage in gospel mortification, the wrath of God is coming.

You will be judged for it." Do you believe that—that we have to give an account for every idle word? That there is a grand assize and a Judge before whom we will stand?

This isn't legalism. Paul is saying that the imperatives are based on the indicatives—but there are imperatives, and this is an imperative: "Put to death therefore what is earthly in you." Are you doing that? Because here's one motivation: the wrath of God is coming.

We see a second motivation in Colossians 3:11. "Here there is not Greek and Jew, circumcised and uncircumcised, barbarian, Scythian, slave, free; but Christ is all, and in all." Paul is saying a number of things here, and among them is that we're all part of a family now. You can't engage in certain activities—activities often involving the tongue: slander and obscene talk, talking about others. Why? Because you're part of a family—the one family of God.

"And above all these put on love, which binds everything together in perfect harmony" (Col. 3:14). There are consequences to our sin—and if we're a part of one family, that means that those consequences involve others. Look at the number of times Paul uses the little expression "one another": "Do not lie to one another" (v. 9); "bearing with one another" (v. 13); "teaching and admonishing one another in all wisdom" (v. 16). You get the picture—one of the motivations for putting sin to death is that we belong to a family. We have obligations to one another. This is the "one-another-ism" of the New Testament.

It's not just about you. I sometimes think that the anthem for Christians is "O say can you see what's in it for me?" We think like that, don't we? *What harm does this do? As long as it doesn't harm anyone else, I can engage in this just a little. Just a little. I can indulge myself—allow myself to think like the world and speak like the world.*

Look at the first items on this list: "Put to death therefore what is earthly in you: *sexual immorality, impurity* . . ." One of the direst threats to the church today is internet pornography. I know you don't want to hear that. Some of you might be shocked at that; most of you are not. It's a reality. Ask any pastor or any elder in the church. The church is riddled with it. It's one of the reasons I think Jesus weeps when he looks down upon his bride. She is an adulterous thing.

Then you notice ". . . covetousness, which is idolatry." Thinking about yourself—that's what this means. It's idolatry. What is sin? Sin is idolatry. It's what the prophets are always saying about Israel's sin: they were always making idols. What does John Calvin say in the *Institutes of the Christian Religion*? That man's mind is a perpetual factory of idols.[2] A graphic image. My favorite television program is *How It's Made*. Little widgets coming off a factory line—that what our mind is like. Idols, one after another. We may be critical of those who worship in an idolatrous fashion—how they bow and genuflect to idols, images, and so on. Well, we have our own idols—all of us. Self-gratification. Lust. Isn't it interesting (and even shocking) that the first thing that Paul mentions here to the church in Colossae is sexual immorality? Well, my dear friend, you belong to a family. You have obligations to your brothers and sisters. Christ died to put away your sins. So each of us must ask, "How can I possibly sin and do this against the family?"

I remember one time in high school after I did something (and it's none of your business just what I did!). My older brother, who is four years older than I, pulled me aside as I was walking down the corridor and took me into a corner. I thought he was going to kill me. He said to me, like some *mafioso* from Sicily, "You're bringing the name of the family into disrepute." This happened about fifty years ago—almost

---

2. See John Calvin, *Institutes of the Christian Religion*, 1.11.8.

half a century—and yet I can hear him say it as though it were yesterday. I was letting the family down. You reap what you sow, and you belong to God's family.

There's yet another motivation: "And whatever you do, in word or deed, do everything in the name of the Lord Jesus, giving thanks to God the Father through him" (v. 17). Everything that you do, do it in the name of the Lord Jesus, because you owe *everything* to him. How can you sin, how can you do these things, and look Jesus in the eye?

The fact is that we kid ourselves. We think we can leave Jesus outside the door for a minute. We can go into a room, we can turn on our computers, we can watch something, and Jesus isn't there. We've left him outside; we'll pick him up on the way out.

In 1 Corinthians 6, Paul does something absolutely shocking. He's talking about fornication—about certain folk in Corinth who were visiting prostitutes. Do you remember what he says? "Do you not know that your bodies are members of Christ? Shall I then take the members of Christ and make them members of a prostitute? Never!" (v. 15). When you sin, you take Jesus with you. You make Jesus enter the places where you're going, you bring Jesus to the things that you do, because you're in union with him. Christ died to put away your sins. He shed his own blood. How can you then sin? That's the motivation—and the strongest possible one. "How can I possibly do this thing that killed the Lord Jesus?"

The Method

There's the mind-set, there are the motives, and now we need to explore a method. Let me suggest three or four things that we see in Colossians 3. First, deprive sin of its opportunity.

Do you remember what happened with Joseph, an attractive young man, when he was tempted by Potiphar's wife? He ran out of the building, leaving his garments in her hands. She cried rape, of course, and he was falsely imprisoned for a number of years. He determined that he would rather endure unjust punishment than sin. "How can I do this thing and sin against my God?" (see Gen. 39:9).

This is a practical measure: cutting off opportunities for sin. What does that mean for us? What it means is that, if you're involved in internet pornography, you need to do some radical things. I was speaking to a young man recently. He's in Christian ministry and got caught up in internet pornography. It's become a habit, and there are triggers that set it off. He is so firmly in the grip of it, in such a habit of it, that he cannot prevent himself from doing it now. I said, "Well, the Congaree River lies three or four blocks from the church. Let's walk down there, and bring your laptop. Let's throw it in the river." He said, "No, no, no, no—I need this! This is part of my work." "Well," I replied, "until you're ready to do that, I can't help you. If this is how serious the habit has become, then you need to deprive yourself of that opportunity. You need to have a computer where everybody can see it. You can't allow yourself to be alone with one. Whatever it takes, deprive yourself of the opportunity. Run. Flee from it."

Since we're talking about method, we also need to learn to oppose sin universally. You notice that Paul gives a list in Colossians 3: "sexual immorality, impurity, passion, evil desire, and covetousness, which is idolatry"—and then a little further down he moves on to "anger, wrath, malice, slander, and obscene talk from your mouth." The first thing I want to point out about this is that sins have names. Just like our pets have names: Lucy, Trigger, Fluffy, Topsy—whatever we call our pets. Sins also have names—individual entities. Here we can slide all too easily into an attitude that says, "Well, so long as I deal with *some* of them." We treat sins like a checklist—one that we look at and say, "Sexual immorality. Well, I'm not guilty of that. Impurity—no, I'm not guilty of that. Passion—no, not guilty of that. Evil desire, covetousness—no, no . . . maybe anger, yes. I'm given to fits of anger and rage. But you know, I've ticked nine of the ten off, so that's OK."

If we're going to follow Paul's recommendation for this, we need to instead oppose sin universally. We need a comprehensive approach to holiness. In Great Britain, for example, when you purchase insurance, you have the option of purchasing "comprehensive insurance," or you can purchase something called "third-party insurance" (which is called "liability" in the United States). With the latter, if you're involved in an accident, you're not covered yourself, but you are covered for the one whom you offend against. Sometimes we approach holiness that way. "As long as other people are involved, I'll take the blame for it." Well, you can't do that, because every sin that you commit has consequences. We belong to a family, remember? Take sexual immorality—you think that it has no consequences for others? Do you think that it has no consequences for yourself?

Here's a third practical thing you can do regarding the method: develop the graces that are contrary to sins. In reality, we can't talk *only* about mortification; we must include vivification, as the two belong together. There are opposites to all of these sins, and we need to concentrate on, develop, promote, and cultivate them. The *no* is essential, but the *yes* is necessary too.

And here's a fourth: be willing to do what is costly. Look at the verb in verse 5: "Put to death." You say, "Well, that's Paul. You know, Paul was kind of austere. He was type A. He was right about everything—difficult to get along with." In that case, let's go to Jesus then. What is Jesus's approach to mortification? "If your right hand causes you to sin, cut it off and throw it away" (Matt. 5:30). Jesus says it is better to go through life with one hand. "If your right eye causes you to sin, tear it out and throw it away" (v. 29). Can you imagine that? I want you to try to imagine putting your fingers in your eye socket and wrenching out your eye. You don't want to think about it, do you?

This is unimaginably horrible to think about it—but that's what Jesus said. That's Jesus's approach to mortification. Kill it. Strangle it. Deprive it of oxygen until it can't breathe and it's dead. Kill sin, or it will kill you. Kill a sin, or part of a sin, every day. That's a measure of your commitment to the Lord Jesus. "Am I dealing with sin? Have I so put it away in a compartment somewhere that I'm no longer dealing with it?" Are you "simply" rejoicing in the grace of the gospel? Well, there are consequences to rejoicing in that grace. There is an ongoing battle with sin. Peter declares,

> But as he who called you is holy, you also be holy in all your conduct, since it is written, "You shall be holy, for I am holy." (1 Peter 1:15–16)

By saying "Put to death" in Colossians 3, Paul isn't talking about definitive sanctification. Rather, he's talking about *progressive* sanctification. He's saying, "You are in a position to do this, now that you have the spiritual resources and the motivations." He's talking to Christians.

What is the evidence, my friend, that you are a Christian? Is there enough evidence to try you and convict you? We have a judge here. Imagine sitting before him, because you're being tried for something, and he has to make a decision. Is there enough evidence to convict this person? You're being tried for being a Christian—for being in union with Christ. Is there enough evidence? One of those pieces of evidence is that you are constantly dealing with indwelling sin. You have to deal with sin for the rest of your life.

I had a tree in the back of my yard in Belfast, where I lived for eighteen years. We were living in the city, and we had a tiny little backyard. The tree had grown to a proportion that was threatening to overtake the entire yard, and I needed to cut it down. I didn't make a great deal of money, and being cheap (as my wife says), I tried to remove it myself. Little by little, I would go out there and hack away at it, starting at the top and working my way down. After several months of this, I reached the stump, took a saw, and sawed it off. I thought, "There. It's done." Then, to my horror, the next spring shoots were coming up out of the ground.

Sin is like that tree. Sometimes you deal with sin and it is gone for the rest of your life—but most likely you're going to have to deal with it over and over and over. Just when you're in your sixties, your seventies, your eighties, and you thought you were done with this sin . . . back it comes. That's when we need to remember the mind-set, the motives, and the method of mortification.

5

Conflict with Evil

ROGER NICOLE

Ephesians 6:10–17

IT IS incumbent upon us to pay close attention to sin—to measure it by the grievousness of our predicament, by the immensity of the remedy that God has provided, and by the final destruction that faces those who are involved in it. It is important for us to note that it is not negative to recognize the gravity of evil.

If you want to deal properly with sin, you have to recognize its gravity, assess its impact, and (especially) grasp the remedy that God has provided. We must always remember that God has never been satisfied with removing the penalty of sin and leaving us exposed to the predicament of sin in our lives. We cannot leave this topic without emphasizing the special way in which God is interested in our struggles. God is interested in overcoming not only the consequences of evil for us but also the very presence and power of evil in us.

This leads us to the emphasis of this chapter: the blessing

of regeneration, which is developed by sanctification and culminates in glorification. But before we grasp this promise, we need to grasp our own situation as pilgrims on this journey—pilgrims who, having been renewed by the grace of God and brought to repentance and a life of faith, now have a life of service and struggle before us. The fact that we have a struggle is made very apparent in this passage from Ephesians 6. The apostle does not say, "As soon as you belong to the Lord Jesus Christ, every problem is resolved, every difficulty smoothed, every propensity of sin subdued." On the contrary, he says that God has called us to a battle royal. He has involved us in the same battle royal in which he has involved himself against the powers of evil in the world.

Knowing Our Enemies

Here in Ephesians 6, the apostle deals first with the question "Who are the enemies?" Second, he asks, "What is it that God calls us to do?" Third, he deals with the question "How has God provided us with the equipment to accomplish what he wants?" So we will consider these three points in turn.

First, who are the enemies? The apostle says, "For we do not wrestle against flesh and blood, but against the rulers, against the authorities, against the cosmic powers over this present darkness, against the spiritual forces of evil in the heavenly places." I understand him to mean not that we don't have to struggle against flesh and blood but that those are not the only enemies we have. The seriousness of the struggle is measured by the fact that, in addition to human powers described by the term "flesh and blood," we have to deal also with celestial powers, demonic powers, satanic powers that are waging war against us. The rest of the Scripture makes it very plain that we have to deal with flesh and blood as well. And it is also true that we have to deal with some remnants of evil within our own nature. Nobody, as long as he or she lives on this earth, is brought to absolute perfection. We are being renewed by the grace of God, but in a gradual manner. And so there is a spiritual growth that is necessary for the children of God. At the time of our regeneration or conversion, we envision some of the things that need to be done—but usually not one tenth of them (or one hundredth). I think that if, when the Lord brings us to himself, we were given a revelation of the full extent of our corruption and evil, we would not survive the shock. All of us would die of shame, disgust, and fear in the presence of the gravity of evil within us.

And so God is gracious to us, revealing our own evil to us only little by little. That is what, I think, people in the Old Testament captured pretty well when they said, "How can I be in the presence of God and live?" If we were really in the presence of the splendor of God's holiness, then our ugliness would really be manifested in all its horror, and this would be so traumatic that we could not survive. We ought not imagine that just because people belong to Christ, have shown repentance and faith, have enlisted themselves in the church, and have received the signs of the covenant, we can therefore expect them to be perfect. Pascal said, "Man is neither angel nor brute, and the unfortunate thing is that he who would act the angel acts the brute."[1] When you imagine that you have finished with evil, that you have nothing wrong with you anymore, that you have reached perfection, you are on a very dangerous downward path. I knew of a man who thought that for twenty years he had not committed a single sin, and he was

---

1. Blaise Pascal, *Pensées*, trans. W. F. Trotter (repr., New York: P. F. Collier & Son, 1910), #358.

boasting about it. I thought to myself, "Isn't it too bad that he should interrupt such a wonderful record!"

Our perfection is not in this life. The Westminster Confession, which is so right on so many subjects, makes that very plain.

> When God converts a sinner, and translates him into the state of grace, he freeth him from his natural bondage under sin; and, by his grace alone, enables him freely to will and to do that which is spiritually good; yet so, as that by reason of his remaining corruption, he doth not perfectly, nor only, will that which is good, but doth also will that which is evil. The will of man is made perfectly and immutably free to good alone, in the state of glory only.[2]

In fact, when people increase in conformity to Jesus Christ, their self-esteem tends to drop down. We find, for instance, the apostle Paul, in his epistle to the Corinthians, being humble enough to see that he was the least of the apostles (see 1 Cor. 15:9), even though he had worked more than them all. Very close to his death, he said, "I am the worst of sinners" (see 1 Tim. 1:15). In fact, he was moving forward, and the image of Christ was being inscribed on his own features more and more. But the more he drew closer to Christ, the more he realized how much he had yet to gain and to progress before the work was actually complete. And so we do have to fight against flesh and blood. We are in danger, and none of us is protected from or immune to sin. And some of the failings of men and women within the church should serve as warnings for all of us. Instead of laughing with those who poke fun at the failings of those in positions of spiritual

---

2. Westminster Confession of Faith, 9.4–5.

leadership—each generation has its Jimmy Swaggarts—we ought to be weeping, because we too are capable of falling and dishonoring the name of Christ. Paul makes this clear in 1 Corinthians 10:12. "Therefore let anyone who thinks that he stands take heed lest he fall." God wants to warn us against the propensity toward evil that is within us—even when we have received him. Even if we have the true salvation that he provides, we are not immune to severe defeats that are disgraceful to the people of God.

Let us not relent in the struggle against the flesh and blood within us. Let us earnestly yearn for God to purge everything that is evil, to put to death that old man that is within us, and to renew us in the image of Jesus Christ as he has promised.

A Threat from Outside: Human Enemies

Our threat is not only from flesh and blood within us but also outside us. We are beset by human enemies who war with us. Indeed, the early Christians—including the Ephesians themselves—had experienced some persecution. We know of human powers that were gathering together and pummeling the church of Jesus Christ in the first and second centuries. Before Constantine's conversion at the beginning of the fourth century, we count ten different serious periods of persecution—some of them extremely severe, and all of them persecutions wherein men and women were called on to give their lives for the testimony of Jesus Christ.

And so there are powers that be that are opposed to Christianity. There are people who hate the very name of Christ—who look at us with envy or disgust just because we are Christians. When they have opportunity to express their dislike, they don't miss the chance. They consider that we are a disagreeable people and that it would be better if we were not around. The apostle Paul emphasizes that these are human powers, and inasmuch as they are human powers, we are not in a position to struggle in a battle royal against them. As Jesus told us, "Love your enemies." Now, please understand—he did not include Satan and the demons in that group. I don't think it's a fulfillment of Christian duty to love Satan and the demons. I don't find that in the Scriptures. These are so identified with evil and sin that there is nothing left to which we could attach our love. But as long as our enemies are human beings, while they are still living we ought to credit the grace of God with the possibility of victory and of their coming to Christ for salvation.

Who was less likely to be elect than the apostle Paul, who persecuted the church? Perhaps there were people in Jerusalem who thought they were free to hate Paul, as he was taking their men and women bound to prison and perhaps to death. And yet this was the very man whom God had chosen to be his instrument of blessing. This was the very man whom God designed to save—out of his own pride, out of his own sin—and designed to incorporate him into the body of Christ and to make him one of the most effective servants of Jesus Christ who has ever lived, as well as the most prolific writer of the New Testament. Paul's words, inspired by the Holy Spirit, have been a source of blessing for all ages and have especially blessed those of us who are the descendants of the Reformers.

And so, as long as people are on the earth, we have not the liberty to wage war against them. We may wage war against some of the things for which they stand, but we have to remember that they are people whom we must love and for whom we must pray.

A Threat from Outside: Demonic Forces

But we must know also that, behind human enemies—
and perhaps using them as their unwitting instruments—there
are demonic powers arrayed against the sovereign power of
God, who intend in every possible way to harm God's people, rip them away from the Good Shepherd (as if that were
even possible), and fling them into destruction, sorrow, and
hell. It is the presence of these demonic powers that caused
the apostle Paul to say, "You are not able to carry on this battle
by yourself. You need supernatural strength to do it." Don't
venture into a battle for which you are wholly unequal; rather,
be strong in the Lord and in his mighty power. It is only the
mighty power of God, manifested by our great champion Jesus
Christ, who on the cross defeated the principalities and powers
and put them to open shame, that will enable the church of
Jesus Christ and every individual to triumph. So we need to be
aware of the subtlety and evil of the demonic powers that are
arrayed against us. The spirit of Satan is abroad and working
feverishly—perhaps because he knows he has little time.

For a long time, in some very real way, it would seem
that Christianized nations like the United States, Canada,
Great Britain, and parts of Western Europe were immune to
certain manifestations of demonic powers. Not many of us
have witnessed exorcisms, in which demons who were actually
possessing a person were expelled in the name of Jesus Christ.

Discerning the presence of demons is a challenging business. Some people who pretend to exorcise at times may not
be entirely trusted to have rightly recognized the presence of
demons in the persons whom they seek to approach. At what
is now Gordon-Conwell Theological Seminary (it was Gordon
Divinity School back then), there was a group of students who
had become very active in the process of exorcism. But they

greatly offended another one of our students whose trailer they exorcised, because they felt that he should not smoke and he was smoking in his own trailer—which was not even on school property. And so they exorcised his trailer—but this did not improve their relationship with him. Because that was the case, they went to the dean's office and proceeded to exorcise him as well! At that point we felt matters had gone a little too far, so we attempted to put the brakes on their form of exorcism. We were not certain they had properly recognized the presence of a demon. Most of us felt there had been an abuse of the principle of exorcism.

Generally, we have been spared the incidents of demon possession that were so frequent in the gospel record. But missionaries have told us some other stories. They have been serving in areas where it indeed seems as though demonic powers are present with great strength. The return of witchcraft, demonism, and Eastern-influenced religions leads us to believe that we have entered a season in which overt demonic activity is quite apparent in the West.

We must be equipped to face and resist whatever may come our way. I have been told, though I have no way of verifying it, that there are 30,000 pastors in West Germany and 90,000 officially registered witches.[3] That means that Germany has three times as many people devoted to witchcraft as people who are at least nominally devoted to the preaching of the Scriptures—and that is in the land of Luther! This is terribly discouraging. And Paul warns us, "You have to wrestle against the rulers, against the authorities, against the cosmic powers over this present darkness, against the spiritual forces of evil in the heavenly places." Those forces of evil took their departure

3. As of 1989, when Nicole delivered this address at the Philadelphia Conference on Reformed Theology.

from heaven, but they still retain some of that supernatural power that God gave them, and they use every ounce of their strength in order to fight against God. Therefore, the Christian really is hard pressed; there is evil within, human evil without, and demonic evil at the back of everything—evil that is militating against his or her best interests.

Stand Therefore

In the presence of this evil, what does God demand that we do? Part of me wants to suggest, "Well, what would someone like General Douglas MacArthur say?" He would say, "You have to pursue the enemy until you have annihilated him. Get after him, follow him wherever he goes, and kill him there." To use the historical analogy of the Korean War, MacArthur would say, "Don't stop at the Yalu River. Don't stop at the 38th Parallel. Keep going until you finally get them out of the way." But it's interesting that we don't see that here in Ephesians. In fact, Paul says the same thing four times, which suggests that he is not using his words haphazardly. He says in verse 11, "Put on the whole armor of God, that you may be able to stand against the schemes of the devil." And again in verse 13, "Therefore take up the whole armor of God, that you may be able to withstand in the evil day, and having done all, to stand firm." And in case we haven't gotten it yet, Paul starts the next verse by saying, "Stand therefore."

At this point, I think we can conclude with some certainty that this is what God wants us to do: to stand. And what would be the opposite of "stand"? Well, clearly "stand" is opposed to "lie down." This is not the time to sleep—to twiddle our thumbs and say, "Well, this is not really a big deal. If the enemy gets much worse, maybe we'll arm ourselves with a weapon or two; but right now we don't need to be worried about it." This is not the time to sit down, either, because that would indicate relaxation. When we read about Jesus Christ as our High Priest, we see that when he had made his offering, *then* he sat down, because the work was accomplished. When your work is accomplished, then you can sit and eat.

God does not tell us to sit down, but to stand. We even have a hymn that says this: "Stand Up, Stand Up for Jesus" by George Duffield Jr. That's what we need to do. God has not demanded of us a direct positive attack, but rather he demands that we stand our ground without being influenced or carried away by the forces of evil. In one way he said that we have to "flee" certain forms of sin, such as sexual immorality, idolatry, and passions of the flesh. But he never said, "Flee Satan." Instead he says, "You stand, and Satan will flee." The fleeing must be Satan's doing, not ours. God wants us to be an army that doesn't yield ground to the power of Satan.

We need people like that today. We need Christians who have the courage of their convictions—who are not afraid to speak up when there's a chance to do so. Christians who will articulate their faith in a manner that, out of conviction rather than out of expediency, is both gentle and forceful. We need Christians who want to be God's instruments against evil. God's orders are clear: "Stand up, people of God, so that the Lord may be magnified, and so victory may come to His forces."

Weapons for War

God did not send us into this struggle without giving us appropriate preparation. In Ephesians 6 we are given a full display of weapons and equipment to use in the battle against Satan. Obviously this is put in terms of the kinds of weapons that were known in those days. While swords and shields would not fare well against machine guns and nuclear bombs, the weaponry that God mentions is clear enough to give us some insight into the nature of the struggle we have. Six weapons are mentioned here in Ephesians, followed by a command to pray that could be considered either as an additional weapon or as the thing that makes all of these weapons effective. Of the six, five weapons are strictly defensive—that is, they are provided to protect the soldier. Only the sword can be used as an offensive weapon.

The weaponry mentioned here is similar to things that we find in Isaiah 11:5 and 59:17. If you examine those passages, you will see that God is the one who is armed. This shows that the weapons of the Christian parallel, in some way, the weapons that God himself wields in his mighty struggle against the power of evil. Moreover, Paul also mentions armament in 1 Thessalonians 5: "But since we belong to the day, let us be sober, having put on the breastplate of faith and love, and for a helmet the hope of salvation" (v. 8). But there is not an exact correspondence between what we find in 1 Thessalonians 5 and what we find in Ephesians. Calvin, the astute exegete that he was, therefore asked the question, "How is it that the description in Thessalonians does not correspond to what we read in Ephesians?" His answer, I think, was very wise:

> [Paul] designs to teach, that the life of Christians is like a perpetual warfare, inasmuch as Satan does not cease to trouble and molest them. He would have us, therefore, be diligently prepared and on the alert for resistance: farther, he admonishes us that we have need of arms, because unless we be well armed we cannot withstand so powerful an enemy. He does not, however, enumerate all the parts of armor. . . . In the meantime, he omits nothing of what belongs

to spiritual armor, for the man that is provided with faith, love, and hope, will be found in no department unarmed.[4]

I don't think it's all that important to discover why salvation is a helmet rather than a breastplate, or why faith is a buckler rather than a belt. You may be aware of the Puritan William Gurnall and of his book *The Christian in Complete Armour*. It is a volume of at least six hundred pages on just two verses in Ephesians 6, so I cannot give a proper account of it in the few pages that remain. In any case, I don't think we are going to benefit much from a discussion about which item covers which part of the body. What is of importance is the nature of the weapons that God has provided. If we forget for a moment what we've read in Ephesians and ask, "What would I list as weapons that God gives me for spiritual warfare?" I dare say we would come up with a very different list than the one Paul presents to us here. We might instead say, "Quick-wittedness, a sharp mind, a resolute will, or great help from our companions in this pilgrimage." These would be the weapons we would think are best suited to equipping us to oppose the enemy.

But that's not what we find in Ephesians. The list of weapons that Paul provides is very different: "Truth, righteousness, zeal for the gospel of peace, faith, salvation." These are the weapons that God has given to us, and every one of them is something he has prepared for us—not something that comes from ourselves. We need to be steeped in the reality of God's grace, which provides for us the equipment we need in order to stand against Satan. God does not say, "Okay—I've put you on your feet. Now go and find the best weapons that you can."

4. John Calvin, *Commentary on The First Epistle to the Thessalonians*, in *Calvin's Commentaries*, vol. 21, *Galatians, Ephesians, Philippians, Colossians, I&II Thess, I&II Timothy, Titus, Philemon* (repr., Grand Rapids: Baker, 2005), 289.

No sir—he has prepared all the weapons for us, and he puts them all at our disposal: The reality of the salvation he has given us. The power of the truth, which must always overcome any power of lies—ultimately no lie can prevail, because the light of the truth will confound it. Faith, which is not a work on our part but is simply an extension of the grace of God. Righteousness, which is not the result of our own good works but is rather imputed to us by virtue of the work of Christ. These are the things that will make us strong, because they will establish us in the grace of the God who has saved us and who equips us so that we are able to stand against the worst attacks of the enemy.

Did you notice? Not a single one of these weapons is intended to cover your back. They are all weapons to cover our front, so that we can extinguish the fiery darts of the enemy as they come against us. If we turn our backs, we are done. If we flee, we've already abandoned the stance that God would have us take. He has not made provision for those who flee; he has made provision for those who stand. The weaponry is in keeping with his orders, and if we disobey these orders we can expect to be undone and to fall victim to the worst attacks of our enemy.

And then, finally, he has given us the Sword of the Spirit, which is the Word of God. How wonderfully God has equipped us there, and how wonderfully our Savior has given us the example of how to wield the Sword of the Spirit against the power of the enemy. Satan tempted Jesus while he was in the desert for forty days and forty nights (see Matt. 4:1–11; Luke 4:1–13). He tempted Jesus first at the lowest level of his life—at the level of hunger, which is such a demanding need in our lives. Hunger is common to all living existence: to animals, plants, humanity—to all living matter. All living things are deprived by hunger.

It is this level of weakness that Satan approached when he said, "Here you are, Jesus! You are dying of hunger! God has just said, 'This is my beloved Son,' and look how he takes care of you—he lets you die of hunger in the desert. Now, if you are the Son of God, use your power! Order those stones to be made into bread. Eat, and sustain yourself."

His appeal here tried to move Jesus to use his own divine power to succor himself in a time of difficulty (which was part of the existence he had accepted as a member of our race). Yet Jesus said, "It is written . . ." He who could have used his own authority to reject Satan took the Sword of the Spirit and said, "Man shall not live by bread alone, but by every word that comes from the mouth of God" (Matt. 4:4). He did the very opposite of Adam, who surrendered to the suggestion of Satan. He did the opposite of the Israelites, who in the desert grumbled against God because they wanted bread and thought he had abandoned them to hunger. It is in connection with that account from Deuteronomy that Jesus makes his response about man not living by bread alone (see Deut. 8:3). The Son of God here uses that passage to say to Satan, "You will not put me off course, Satan, because I use the Word of God, and you must yield to it." Satan knew that he was beaten on that point.

He continues his attack by taking Jesus to a high mountain. "You want to win the world? I'll give you an easy way. You don't have to go by the way of the cross. You don't have to suffer that awful ordeal. All you have to do is surrender to my authority. You bend down to me and I'll give you all of it, because it all belongs to me." Of course, it wasn't his anyway—but Satan has never been finicky about how big or how small a lie he presents. Yet Jesus answered, "It is written, 'You shall worship the Lord your God, and him only shall you serve'" (Luke 4:8).

Satan again knew that he was beaten, but now he said to

himself, "This Sword of the Spirit is awfully effective. I wonder if I can use it, too." So he took Jesus to the pinnacle of the temple and said, "Jesus, why don't you make a big display of your power right there in front of the people? They will receive you. Jump down from there, for it is written, 'He will command his angels concerning you, to guard you,' and 'On their hands they will bear you up, lest you strike your foot against a stone'" (see Luke 4:10)." He was referring to Psalm 91 when he said, "It is written . . ." And that's true—it's there. Those words are indeed written in Psalm 91:11–12. Note that Jesus didn't say in response, "Well, that's a psalm that comes from a Maccabean period, and biblical critics are going to cast some doubt on its value." His question was not about whether it was written but about whether it could be interpreted that way. And so he tells Satan that it is *also* written, "You shall not put the Lord your God to the test" (Luke 4:12). And Satan retired, defeated.

Three times the Sword of the Spirit brought Satan low— three times the Lord Jesus, who had all the power in the world to respond, used the very same weapon that he has placed into our hands. When Satan comes to us with doubting questions— about whether the Scriptures are inspired, about whether we can really trust an old book, about whether the critics have not undermined the value of Deuteronomy, Job, or whatever other book—send him back to Jesus! Tell Satan, "Why didn't you tell that to Jesus in the desert, when he was sending you reeling on your back with a simple word of Scripture?"

Using the Sword of the Spirit

God has given us the Sword of the Spirit, which is the Word of God, and there is no superior weapon that Satan can forge against the servant or maidservant of Jesus Christ who wields it. God does not send us into this battle unprepared or unarmed. He has given us all the equipment that we might desire. He has prepared us for the battle.

I would like to close with a passage from *Pilgrim's Progress*. We pick up with an episode in the story of Pilgrim's wife, Christiana, and her guide Mr. Great-heart, who had himself just struggled against three enemies known as Wildhead, Inconsiderate, and Pragmatic.

> Then they went on; and . . . there stood a man with his sword drawn, and his face all bloody. Then said Mr. Great-heart, "Who art thou?" The man-made answer, saying, "I am one whose name is Valiant-for-truth. I am a pilgrim, and am going to the Celestial City." Now, as I was in my way, there were three men did beset me, and propounded unto me these three things: 1. Whether I would become one of them? 2. Or go back to the place from whence I came? 3. Or die upon the place? To the first I answered, I had been a true man a long season, and therefore it could not be expected that I should now cast in my lot with thieves. Then they demanded what I should say to the second. So I told them that the place from whence I came, had I not found it unsatisfactory I had not forsaken at all; but, finding it altogether unsuitable to me, and very unprofitable for me, I forsook it for this way. Then they asked me what I said to the third. And I told them my life cost more dear far than that I should lightly give it away. Besides you have nothing to do thus to put things to my choice, wherefore at your peril be it if you meddle. Then these three, to wit, Wildhead, Inconsiderate, and Pragmatic, drew their weapons upon me, and I also drew upon them. So we fell to it, one against three, for the space of above three hours. They have

left upon me, as you see, some of the marks of their valor, and have also carried away with them some of mine. They are but just now gone: I suppose they might, as the saying is, hear your horse dash, and so they betook them to flight."

Great. But here was great odds, three against one.

Valiant. 'Tis true; but little or more are nothing to him that has the truth on his side. "Though an host should encamp against me," said one, "my heart shall not fear: though war should rise against me, in this will I be confident. Besides," said he, "I have read in some records that one man has fought an army; and how many did Samson slay with the jaw-bone of an ass?"

Great. Then said the guide, "Why did you not cry out, that some might have come in for your succor?"

Valiant. So I did, to my King, who, I knew, could hear me, and afford invisible help; and that was sufficient for me.

Great. Then said Great-heart to Mr. Valiant-for-truth, "Thou hast worthily behaved thyself. Let me see thy sword." So he showed it him. When he had taken it in his hand, and looked thereon a while, he said, "Ha! It is a right Jerusalem blade."

Valiant. It is so. Let a man have one of these blades, with a hand to wield it and skill to use it, and he may venture upon an angel with it. He need not fear its holding, if he can but tell how to lay on. Its edges will never blunt. It will cut flesh and bones, and soul and spirit, and all.

Great. But you fought a great while. I wonder you were not weary.

Valiant. I fought till my sword did cleave to my hand; and when they were joined together, as if a sword grew out of my arm, and when the blood ran through my fingers, then I fought with most courage.

Great. Thou hast done well; thou hast resisted unto

blood, striving against sin. Thou shalt abide by us, come in and go out with us, for we are thy companions.[5]

That is the true destiny of the Christian: to be Mr. or Mrs. Valiant-for-Truth, having the Sword of the Spirit so tight, so close, that it is almost as if it grew out of his or her arm. As long as we are on this earth, we are engaged in this struggle. Yet the time will come, in the gracious purpose of God, when all evil will be subdued and when every presence of evil will be erased both from our souls and from our bodies. When all the enemies that Satan can muster will be defeated and will be sent to a place where they cannot reach us nor harm us. When Jesus Christ will at last present his church as a bride without blemish, wrinkle, or stain. It is then that we will sing, again and again, as in the words of Handel's *Messiah*, "Hallelujah!" Amen.

5. John Bunyan, *The Pilgrim's Progress* (repr., Edinburgh, UK: Banner of Truth Trust, 2017), 348–50.

6

Deliverance from the Evil One

R. KENT HUGHES

Ephesians 2:1–10

SOME YEARS ago—in fact, many, many years ago—I was a youth pastor in southern California. One day, I got together with some of the young men in my high school group, and together we decided to climb Mount Whitney—the highest point in the continental United States (14,505 feet). We drove out in the middle of the night, parked our car at about 7,000 feet, and pitched our tent at 11,000 feet, and the next day we ascended to the top of Mount Whitney. It was a glorious day. We were at the peak of the Sierra Nevada mountain range, looking down to the Mojave Desert and the turquoise lakes below. Vista on vista on vista stretched toward the horizons. It was a fantastic place to be.

As we gazed together from what seemed the top of the

world, one of the young men said, "You know, 80 miles away, that's Death Valley to the southeast, and it is the lowest place in the United States—some 280 feet below sea level. Death Valley had the hottest recorded temperature in the United States: 134 degrees Fahrenheit in the shade." What a contrast—one place was at the top of the world, the other at the bottom. One perpetually cool, the other relentlessly hot.

In Ephesians 2, Paul takes us down into the Death Valley of the soul (vv. 1–3) and then brings us up to the heavenly places in Christ Jesus (vv. 4–7). His method is contrast: from death to life, from hell to heaven, from bondage to freedom, from pessimism to optimism. The great contrast that we have here in Ephesians 2 helps us to really appreciate our deliverance from Satan—our deliverance from bondage to life.

The Death Valley of the Soul

Paul begins at the very bottom of the valley: "And you were dead in . . . trespasses and sins" (v. 1). That is an absolute statement. Paul doesn't mean that the Ephesians were merely in danger of death, but that they were in a state of death—present death. It's not a figure of speech; they were absolutely dead. He begins by referring to Gentiles, but down in verse 3 he includes Israel and himself as well. He's not talking about some drugged, decadent society; he's talking about all of humanity, from top to bottom. All people are dead apart from Christ. When Paul says "dead," he means death universally, absolutely, and without exception.

I have a photograph of the philosopher Jeremy Bentham—the father of utilitarianism. It's a picture of his corpse, seated in a chair and wearing the top hat of a gentlemen of the 19th century—it/he rests in a glass case in London's University College

Hospital. You can go see it today—you could even set this book down and look it up online (but you wouldn't do that, right?).

The story is told that, up until recently, Bentham's body would be wheeled out in its chair to a board meeting once a year, and then the president of the board says, "Jeremy Bentham, present but not voting." It's a big joke; he will never raise his hand and he will never vote, because he's been dead since 1832.

The fact is that dead people can't do anything. This is what Paul means when he talks about the spiritual state of those who are apart from Christ. But how can this be? When we look out at people around us, their bodies are virile and healthy. They have quick, active intellects, and many are overflowing with personality. They possess the full range of human emotions. But in the place where it matters most—in the soul—they have no life. They are blind to the reality and glory of Christ, and they do not love him. They are as deaf to the Holy Spirit as a corpse. As John Stott once said, "We should not hesitate to reaffirm that a life without God (however physically fit and mentally alert the person may be) *is a living death*, and those who live it are dead even while they're living."[1] They're in Death Valley.

Those are hard, hard words—especially hard and offensive words in the light of our culture today. Paul says that those who are spiritually dead are "following the course of this *world*, following the *prince of the power of the air*, the spirit that is now at work in the sons of disobedience—among whom we all once lived in the *passions of our flesh*, carrying out the desires of the body and the mind, and were by nature children of wrath, like the rest of mankind" (Eph. 2:2–3). This is the order that Paul

---

1. John R. W. Stott, *God's New Society: The Message of Ephesians* (Downers Grove, IL: IVP, 1979), 72.

gives in the text: the world, the devil, and the flesh. "World" here is the word *kosmos*, which is used 186 times in the Greek New Testament and always with a reference to evil. Here Paul means that the spiritually dead follow the course of the present evil age. That is how we walked before Christ. Those who are without Christ are captive to the social value systems of the present age and are hostile to God. They are willing slaves of the media, group think, talk shows, post-Christian mores, and standard religious fads. They are dead.

Paul then describes the devil as "the prince of the power of the air, the spirit that is now at work in the sons of disobedience." Satan is described in various ways throughout Scripture: as the "ancient serpent" (Rev. 20:2), the "ruler of this world" (John 12:31), the "prince of demons" (Matt. 9:34), and, perhaps most alarming, the "god of this world" (2 Cor. 4:4).

Luther's magnificent term from "A Mighty Fortress Is Our God" really does capture it: he calls our adversary the "Prince of Darkness Grim." As the prince of the power of the air, Satan commands an almost innumerable army of demonic allies. How do we know that? Paul supplies an explanation in Ephesians 6:12: "For we do not wrestle against flesh and blood, but against the rulers, against the authorities, against the cosmic powers over this present darkness, against the spiritual forces of evil in the heavenly places." Paul is talking about angelic rulers, authorities, cosmic powers, and spiritual forces of evil, indicating a vast organized hierarchy.[2] F. F. Bruce thinks this is a reference to high-ranking fallen angels, such as the angel princes of Persia and Greece that opposed the archangel in the book of Daniel.[3] Whatever their exact designation, these

2. The word translated "cosmic powers" is *kosmokratóras*. If you wish, you can translate it into English as "cosmocrats."
3. See F. F. Bruce, *The Epistle to the Ephesians* (repr., London: Pickering & Inglis, 1973), 128.

powers present a great demonic enemy with a defined, disciplined chain of command.

We don't want to trivialize this, thinking that these are just a group of winged opossums flying around. This is an intellectual, intelligent, wicked, angelic elite. Though the devil can be only one place at a time, with his myriad of malignant spirits he imitates (albeit imperfectly) God's omnipresence and omnipotence. He wants to be God. The consensus of Scripture is that the world is the devil's world (*cosmos diabolicus*, to use the Latin term). "We know that we are from God, and the whole world lies in the power of the evil one" (1 John 5:19).

So we see the world and the devil—but then there's more: our flesh (see Eph. 2:3). The dead—those who are without Christ—are corrupted from within, too.[4] They are dominated by the world, the devil, and the flesh. The world dominates from without, the flesh from within, and the devil from beyond. These are the terrible dynamics of spiritual death.

Our Status: Children of Wrath

Then Paul concludes, in Ephesians 2:3, "We . . . were by nature children of wrath, like the rest of mankind." Everyone—Jews and Gentiles—were and are sinners by nature, because we all sinned in and with Adam. That's what we are. John 3:36 is stark on this point: "Whoever believes in the Son has eternal life; whoever does not obey the Son shall not see life, but the wrath of God remains on him."

---

4. I love this story: A little girl was being disciplined by her mother for kicking her brother in the shins and pulling his hair. Mom said to her little girl, "Sally, why did you let the devil make you kick your little brother in the shins and pull his hair?" Sally answered, "The devil made me kick him, but pulling the hair was my idea."

What Paul writes early in Ephesians 2 actually serves as a synopsis of what we find in the first three chapters of Romans—chapters that teach the total depravity and death of humankind.

This needs to be said, because the truth has been forgotten: the biblical doctrine of depravity means that every part of the human person is tainted by sin. This doesn't mean that all humans are *equally* depraved in their depth; most don't go near the depths of sin to which they could go. As John Gerstner once said, "There's always room for *deprovement*."[5] Does this mean that humans are not capable of any good—that there's no dignity in man? Absolutely not; humans are still God's image bearers (see Gen. 1:27). But even so, there is no part of the human being—the mind, the emotions, the heart, the will—that remains unaffected by the fall. All of us are totally depraved.

Because of this depravity, we are totally lost. So profound is the human predicament that, near the end of his argument in Romans 3, Paul says, "None is righteous, no, not one; no one understands; no one seeks for God" (Rom. 3:10–11). Paul, who was steeped in Old Testament theology, was drawing from Psalm 14:

> The LORD looks down from heaven on the children of man,
>   to see if there are any who understand,
>   who seek after God.
>
> They have all turned aside; together they have become
>   corrupt;
>   there is none who does good,
>   not even one. (Ps. 14:2–3)

5. John H. Gerstner, "The Atonement and the Purpose of God," *Tenth Quarterly*, July 1978, 5.

They don't even seek God. People may seek health; they may seek well-being; they may seek other things. But apart from the prompting of the Holy Spirit, they do not seek God. Absolute spiritual death. The Jeremy Bentham principle.

Turning Upward

That's enough depression for one chapter—now we're going to change direction to an upward bent. The journey from Death Valley to the spiritual heights is accomplished only by one thing, and that is resurrection: "But God, being rich in mercy, because of the great love with which he loved us, even when we were dead in our trespasses, made us alive together with Christ" (Eph. 2:4–5). Man is radically dead, and he can be saved only by the radicalness of resurrection. If you're a believer, that's what you have experienced.

I remember sitting down to dinner with a colleague of mine, Dr. William Edgar, who serves as professor of apologetics at Westminster Theological Seminary in suburban Philadelphia. Bill told my wife and me about how he had been witnessed to by Harold O. J. Brown when he was an undergraduate student at Harvard. He soon began to be interested in spiritual things. The following summer, Edgar traveled to Europe, to his father's business in Switzerland, and he soon realized that he wasn't far from where Francis Schaeffer was in L'Abri.[6] He visited L'Abri, and within twenty-four hours Edgar was absolutely given new life and was spiritually resurrected from the dead. That event changed his whole life—he was made alive by the resurrection.

At that moment, what Bill Edgar experienced was also an ascension: "[God] raised us up with him and seated us with him

6. A French word meaning "the shelter."

in the heavenly places in Christ Jesus" (Eph. 2:6). What is true about Dr. Edgar is also true about you if you know Christ. While we may not physically be present "in the heavenly places," we Christians are already in the heavenlies by virtue of our union with Christ. Spiritually, we are seated with him on the throne along with other believers, and the powers of the spiritual realm have been brought to bear in our lives in this present age.

One of my favorite texts is Hebrews 12:22–24—a passage that provides for us a "seven wonders" of the church. It gives us a glimpse into what we've inherited:

> But you have come to Mount Zion and to the city of the living God, the heavenly Jerusalem, and to innumerable angels in festal gathering, and to the assembly of the first-born who are enrolled in heaven, and to God, the judge of all, and to the spirits of the righteous made perfect, and to Jesus, the mediator of a new covenant, and to the sprinkled blood that speaks a better word than the blood of Abel.

We are firstborn heirs to the assembly of *the* firstborn. Enrolled in heaven, we are joint heirs with Jesus Christ. We have come to God, who is the judge of all men; to the Church triumphant; to the spirits of the righteous made perfect; to Jesus, the mediator of a new covenant; and to sprinkled blood that speaks a better word than the blood of Abel, as it shouts "Forgiveness!"

What will be the end of all this? There is no end! ". . . so that in the coming ages [God] might show the immeasurable riches of his grace in kindness toward us in Christ Jesus" (Eph. 2:7). That is, in the unfolding ages there will be unfolding grace, after grace, after grace, after grace, after grace—the kind of thing that would indeed make the fallen angels green with envy.

On the Pinnacle

My friends and I stood on the pinnacle of Mount Whitney, rejoicing in all the beauty we were witnessing. Just then, a fighter jet shot by. It had evidently come from a naval air base nearby in the Mojave. The pilot thought he would have a good time and buzz the top of Mount Whitney. We saw this jet coming right at us, with all kinds of gray smoke streaming out of its exhaust. As he sped over us, he broke the sound barrier before barrel-rolling off into the horizon. Then he came back straight across us and repeated the same maneuver.

I don't think his superiors knew what he was doing, but we did. He was just an observer passing by in a plastic bubble—a sonic plastic bubble. But we were *there*, standing on the summit, breathing the Alpine freshness, feeling God's creation. The only thing that would have made the occasion better is if we had started in Death Valley that morning before climbing to the summit of Whitney so we'd experience the contrast.

Believers, we have done that very thing in Christ. We were all in the Death Valley of the soul—lost, desolate, hopeless. Now, through resurrection, we have been raised to the highest heaven, and we are fully alive. That resurrection power is available for all those who are without life—even among the parched bones of Death Valley.

I've said a lot about Death Valley. You might recall another death valley in the book of Ezekiel:

> The hand of the LORD was upon me, and he brought me out in the Spirit of the LORD and set me down in the middle of the valley; it was full of bones. And he led me around among them, and behold, there were very many on the surface of the valley, and behold, they were very dry. And he said to me, "Son of man, can these bones live?" And I

answered, "O Lord GOD, you know." Then he said to me, "Prophesy over these bones, and say to them, O dry bones, hear the word of the LORD. Thus says the Lord GOD to these bones: Behold, I will cause breath to enter you, and you shall live. And I will lay sinews upon you, and will cause flesh to come upon you, and cover you with skin, and put breath in you, and you shall live, and you shall know that I am the LORD. (Ezek. 37:1–6)

When Ezekiel did as God instructed, those bones came rattling together, the sinews came back into place, and skin formed over them. "So I prophesied as he commanded me, and the breath came into them, and they lived and stood on their feet, an exceedingly great army" (v. 10). Reader, we need—humanity needs—that new life that comes only from God's grace.

From Hell to Heaven

Paul has taken us from hell to heaven, bondage to freedom, gloom to light, despair to hope, wrath to glory, and death to life. Now Paul is at the magnificent pinnacle. He's not 15,000 feet high and looking down on the Mojave Desert; he's standing on the pinnacle of heaven. He pauses to catch his breath, and then he recapitulates, in these brief but immortal words from the mountaintop:

> For by grace you have been saved through faith. And this is not your own doing; it is the gift of God, not a result of works, so that no one may boast. (Eph. 2:8–9)

I have this underlined in my Bible, and perhaps you have it underlined in yours. That statement is the most cogent summary of the dynamics of salvation to be found anywhere in Scripture. So many people have come to Christ over these words. I've seen so many tears fall as a man or a woman or a child is regenerated upon hearing these words. You've seen it yourself—readers of these words have gone from death to life.

In a sense, I'm likely preaching to the choir. Yet there are always some who are delightful interlopers—visitors (so to speak) who are hearing (or reading) the gospel from the outside. To you, I say this: what you need to do right now is shut everything out, all the distractions, and give attention to these gospel words: *"For by grace you have been saved through faith. And this is not your own doing; it is the gift of God, not a result of works, so that no one may boast."*

I must admit that I wasn't saved upon hearing that text. I was saved through a different text that I read out of a little Bible many years ago. I had been attending a church where I heard the gospel preached. I felt like I was on the outside looking in. I felt that salvation could never happen to me; I doubted that I could know what those people knew and have a life that those people had. I was twelve years old, but that's what I thought. Then I heard a sermon preached and I went up to the preacher. He sat down with me, and I opened this little Bible that my grandmother had given to me—signed to me on my seventh birthday. I read these words in the King James Version: "That if thou shalt confess with thy mouth the Lord Jesus, and shalt believe in thine heart that God hath raised him from the dead, thou shalt be saved" (Rom. 10:9). And I believed it. It was as if those words came right up into my eyes, into my mind, and into my heart, and I was regenerated. I was spiritually resurrected. I was born again. Though I was only twelve years old, I went from Death Valley to the pinnacle *by the grace of God.*

If you just step back and look at Ephesians 2, you see

amazing depths (vv. 1–3), amazing heights (vv. 4–7), amazing grace (vv. 8–9), and then amazing work: "For we are his workmanship, created in Christ Jesus unto good works, which God hath before ordained that we should walk in them" (v. 10 KJV). This is all God. We are his workmanship, his masterpiece, created unto good works to follow him. As you read these words from God's inerrant Word, may the grace of God elevate your souls and cause you to love him more with all your being. May we serve him as he's called us and elected us to do.

7

Persevering in Satan's Sieve

JOEL R. BEEKE

Luke 22:31–32

A COUPLE whose marriage I had performed wanted to meet with me again a few years later, and when we did, the woman said, "I want a divorce."

"You want a divorce? Why?" I asked.

"Well, he's not meeting all my needs."

"My dear friend, what makes you think that a mortal man could meet all your needs? Marriage wasn't designed for that—only Christ can meet all your needs!"

The beauty, you see, of persevering in Christ's strength—of holding fast to him who holds us fast—is that it's all to be found in the offices that Christ bears as our Prophet, Priest, and King: roles that provide the model and mentorship for their earthly counterparts. It's Jesus's prophetical, priestly, royal ministry that gives us the grace to persevere, even in the sieve of Satan.

In Luke 22, the disciples are arguing over who is the greatest. This is astonishing, considering that it comes right after the first administration of the Lord's Supper. Jesus tells them that they shouldn't be arguing and should instead be serving one another. He continues,

> And I appoint unto you a kingdom, as my Father hath appointed unto me; That ye may eat and drink at my table in my kingdom, and sit on thrones judging the twelve tribes of Israel. (vv. 29–30)

This brings us to his words found in the reference at the beginning of this chapter, along with Peter's response:

> And the Lord said, Simon, Simon, behold, Satan hath desired to have you, that he may sift you as wheat: But I have prayed for thee, that thy faith fail not: and when thou art converted, strengthen thy brethren. And he said unto him, Lord, I am ready to go with thee, both into prison, and to death. And he said, I tell thee, Peter, the cock shall not crow this day, before that thou shalt thrice deny that thou knowest me. (vv. 31–34)

I want to approach this topic of how Jesus meets all our needs through his office-bearing along the following three lines: Jesus's prophetic admonition, his priestly intercession, and his kingly commission.

Prophetic Admonition

The disciples have just commemorated the Lord's Supper with Jesus. They're coming off a distinct highlight. "But, behold, the hand of him that betrayeth me is with me on the table" (v. 21). Jesus now confronts his own disciples with the cruel temptations of the devil. The frightening truth is that the disciples are not aware of Satan's presence, but the comforting truth is that Jesus is. Jesus knows that when he, the good and the great and the chief shepherd, will be smitten, the sheep will be scattered, and Satan will attack them like a wolf. But Jesus also knows that he will continue praying for them.

But notice that he particularly warns Simon Peter, as if to say, "Simon, Satan has his sights on you." A nineteenth-century preacher put it this way: "It is almost as though Satan spoke thus—'I have picked off one of the lieutenants; let me see if I cannot shoot down the colonel. I have got Judas; I will have Peter next.'"[1] You see, Satan aims for leaders first and foremost. I had a woman in my congregation who was on a plane and was sitting next to someone who was praying. After he was done, she said to him, "I see you're a Christian."

"No, I'm not a Christian," the man replied.

"Oh—well, I thought you were praying."

"Well, I was praying . . . to the devil."

"The devil?! Why would you ever pray to the devil?"

"I was praying that the devil would separate thirty pastors from their congregations and bring them to downfall this week in America."

---

1. J. C. Philpot, "The Sieve and Its Effects" (sermon, Providence Chapel, London, July 16, 1849), available online at https://www.gracegems.org /Philpot/sieve_and_its_effects.htm.

"Pastor," she said afterward as she recounted this incident to me, "the most frightening thing was that he looked more earnest as he was praying than I feel in my prayers." You see, Satan wants to have us—and particularly us ministers—because of our past usefulness, our present position, and our potential value. If you are a church leader of any kind, or if you're involved in any ministry—even to your children—Satan wants you. He declares holy war (*jihad*) on those who serve Christ in his kingdom.

"Simon, Simon, behold" is really a triple warning. If I call one of my children by name twice, using a certain tone of voice, they know that I mean business. How much more so if Jesus does this! This is the third time in Luke's gospel that Jesus repeats someone's name: "Martha, Martha" (10:41), "Jerusalem, Jerusalem" (13:34), and now "Simon, Simon." The third emphasis of warning follows: "Behold." It's meant to shake Peter up. "Pay attention! Wake up!" our Lord says. "What I'm about to say is important: Satan wants you. Satan will use every weapon in his arsenal to destroy your ministry—to discredit the gospel of Jesus Christ."

John Calvin put it this way: "[The ministry] is no pleasant occupation, in which we may exercise ourselves agreeably and with delight of heart, but a hard and severe warfare . . . [with] Satan from time to time giving us as much trouble as he can, and leaving no stone unturned to annoy us."[2] Richard Baxter was even stronger: "[Satan] knows what a rout he may make among the [troops], if the leaders fall before their eyes. He hath long tried that way of fighting, 'neither against great nor small' comparatively, but . . . of 'smiting the

2. John Calvin, *Commentary on The Second Epistle to the Corinthians*, in *Calvin's Commentaries*, vol. 20, *I Corinthians, II Corinthians* (repr., Grand Rapids: Baker, 2005), 362.

shepherds, that he may scatter the flock.' And so great hath been his success this way, that he will follow it on as far as he is able."[3]

The frightening truth about Satan is that he knows us. He observes our character, moment by moment, and he knows our weakest points. Isn't that true in your life? Haven't you noticed that the things that you easily stumble over surface repeatedly? Satan keeps presenting them to you, and you often fall so easily that it's embarrassing.

Many summers ago, my son talked me into going fishing. I hadn't been fishing for forty years. No sooner had I managed to cast my line into the fast-moving river before I reeled in a fifteen-inch-long walleye. It was great! I pulled it in and thought, *Wow, I'm going to catch a lot of fish!*

Other fishermen commented, "You caught a walleye in this river? What did you use?"

"A worm," I said.

"You caught a walleye with just a measly worm?"

The point, you see, is that the walleye doesn't normally allow himself to be caught by a little worm—yet this one stumbled so easily. We sometimes do the same—in our weakness, we stumble over measly little worms. My friend, may I warn you in the words of Jesus today, "Simon, Simon, behold." Don't eat the little worms of this world in the place of the Lord Jesus Christ!

How faithful Christ is to Peter here—and how faithful our friends are to us when they point out our weak points. "Faithful are the wounds of a friend" (Prov. 27:6). May I ask you to seriously consider this? Satan wants you.

Do you remember those old posters in the post office

---

3. Richard Baxter, *The Reformed Pastor: Showing the Nature of the Pastoral Work* (1656; repr., London, n.d.), 32.

with Uncle Sam in his flag-draped hat and his bony finger pointing out, as the poster reads, "Uncle Sam wants YOU"? Satan is pointing at us. He wants *me*, and he also wants *you*. And so he puts temptation all along our road.

And still, Peter just brushes aside all these warnings. "Lord," he says, "I am ready to go with thee, both into prison, and to death" (v. 33). You see, he wasn't shaken by the seriousness of Christ's words—and apparently not even by the fall of Judas.

Satan is a murderer from the beginning, a liar from the beginning, the Judas from among the angels, the great apostate, the angel who rebelled. This archenemy of God can no longer reach Christ, so he's expending his energies to destroy the image of Christ in people like you and me. Be aware, and be prophetically admonished by the loving warning of Jesus Christ.

So what does Satan want to do with us? Well, he wants to shake us—to sift us, Jesus says, "as wheat." What does that mean? It means that he wants to do to you as a farmer does to his grain. In Bible times, a farmer's threshing floor contained both wheat and chaff. The farmhand would take a large sieve and scoop up the mixture of material on the threshing floor. He would then shake it back and forth so that the dirt would fall to the ground, and then he'd shake it up and down so that the straw and chaff would come to the surface. Then he would reach in and pull away the straw and chaff, and all that would be left in the sieve would be pure wheat.

What Satan wants to do, however, is to shake you so that the chaff and the straw come to the surface and choke the pure grain. Satan seeks to destroy you—to checkmate you. Perhaps you have heard of that famous piece of art in a European art gallery that's simply titled *The Chess Players*.[4] It depicts a game

---

4. Editor's note: *Die Schachspieler* in German. The painting is by

of chess—on one side we see a man who looks like Satan, with a gleeful look in his eyes. Across from him sits a young man who is holding his head in agony, about to be checkmated. Satan wants to strangle the work of God in you—to put you in checkmate. He wants to sift you as wheat; he wants to destroy you in his sieve.

Most of us, I'm afraid, don't do very well in Satan's sieve, even if we've been followers of Jesus Christ for a long time. Sometimes I am so disappointed in myself. I've been a Christian now for several decades, and sometimes I act as if I've been saved for only a few months—or maybe not at all. How tragic! I should be so much more mature, so much further along than I am.

Then I turn to the Bible and see that biblical saints often had the same problem. In Satan's sieve, Abraham twice says, "Sarah is my sister" (see Gen. 12:13; 20:2). Jacob gets in Satan's sieve and says, "All these things are against me" (Gen. 42:36). Job gets in Satan's sieve and, after responding so well at first, says, "Let the day perish wherein I was born" (Job 3:3).

My friend, in our flesh there dwells no good thing (see Rom. 7:18). We are proud, selfish, and unbelieving by nature; we backslide easily. "For the good that I would I do not: but the evil which I would not, that I do" (Rom. 7:19). We are so vulnerable to Satan. Satan is cunning and resourceful; he can outlive us, outwork us, outwit us. "The heart is deceitful above all things, and desperately wicked: who can know it?" (Jer. 17:9).

Do you ever feel like Satan is one step ahead of you? There's a story of a watermelon farmer whose watermelons were being stolen by thieves. One day the farmer finally said, "I'll fix those thieves." So he put a sign in his watermelon

---

Friedrich Moritz August Retzsch (1779–1857).

patch that said, "WARNING: one of these watermelons is poisoned." Over the next two weeks, no watermelons were taken; but then the farmer noticed that a sign had been placed next to his own sign: "WARNING: two of these watermelons are poisoned." The farmer had to throw away his whole patch of watermelons. You see, as soon as you think that you have Satan, he's got you. "Simon, Simon, behold, Satan hath desired to have you, that he may sift you as wheat." We need to take this warning seriously. We need to be aware of Satan's devices and expect him to work against us. It should be no surprise to us—this is his business, after all. Thank Jesus for his loving, prophetical warnings in our lives. His very warnings help to meet our needs.

Priestly Intercession

But thanks be to God that our text does not end with Luke 22:31. "Satan hath desired to have you, that he may sift you as wheat: *But I have prayed for thee*, that thy faith fail not" (vv. 31–32). Our prophetic Admonisher is also our priestly Intercessor, and he sets up Satan's desires against his own desires. It's remarkable—the word that's used here is *exaiteō*, an intensified form of the word meaning "to ask" or "to pray." It can best be translated as "I *myself* have prayed for thee."

Satan asks emphatically for you; he wants to sue God's courts for you, almost as he did with Job. "I want to *have* Job," Satan says as he dialogues with God. But Jesus responds, "Though Satan asks emphatically for you, I also ask for you in the strongest possible way. He puts in a claim, but I put in a counterclaim."

Jesus declares, "Satan's only claim to have you is that you're a sinner; that you're unworthy of God; that you're worthy of hell; that you're not as faithful as you ought to be; that you don't deserve to stand. But my counterclaim is better! My claim is that I myself have been in Satan's sieve, and I have gone through it sinlessly. I have gained the victory, and I am going to the cross to lay down my life in order to earn the right to have you, to possess you, to merit your salvation, and to call you, and to keep you as my own!"

What encouraging, astonishing grace! The Lord of Glory, the sinless Creator of the heavens and earth, would come to this lowly place called earth to "be sin for us, who knew no sin; that we might be made the righteousness of God in him" (2 Cor. 5:21). Jesus perseveres in Satan's sieve—he perseveres to the end, setting his face like a flint toward Jerusalem (see Luke 9:51; cf. Isa. 50:7). Jesus, knowing all things that would come upon him, went forth—because he loves his Father's will and because he loves his people and will not let them go.

Isn't that wonderful? He keeps the feet of his saints; his prayers are effectual and almighty—mightier than Satan's. Thanks be to God! Satan is mightier than we are, but Jesus is mightier than Satan is. Satan is a fallen angel; Jesus is the living God of heaven and earth, and all power is given unto him.

"I myself have prayed for thee." Think of it: in those last dreadful hours, as Jesus is about to walk through the valley of Gethsemane and Gabbatha and Golgotha, where all the powers of hell will be unleashed—in that hour, Jesus says to Simon Peter, "You're brushing off my warning; but *I myself pray for thee*, that thy faith fail not."

Thank God for the intercession of Jesus. I have often said to my seminary students that I think the intercession of Jesus is one of the most minimized doctrines in all the Bible. Without the intercession of Jesus, I wouldn't be standing here today. I'd be in the bottom of hell, and so would you. He keeps us, moment by moment by moment. Christ ever lives to make intercession for us (see Rom. 8:34; Heb. 7:25). Is that truth precious to you? I don't know about you, but I've had times in my life when I've crawled on the ground, crying out for relief, crying out for deliverance, crying out until I couldn't cry anymore—and sometimes until I couldn't pray anymore. Sometimes the only word that was left was "Lord"—and sometimes not even that. How glorious to know that he is praying for me even when I cannot. Oh the power, the security, the joy, the comfort of knowing that I have a Savior who won't forget me! There's nothing like it in all the world.

And what does he pray for us? "That thy faith fail not." Notice that Jesus doesn't pray that Peter won't enter into Satan's sieve; nor does he pray that Peter's abilities or self-confidence won't fail. He prays only that Peter's *faith* will not fail. Why faith? Because faith centers wholly and exclusively on Jesus. You see, Jesus is actually using Satan to further Peter's spiritual maturity. Peter's sin and fall were terrible, and we don't want to minimize that in any way. But Jesus overruled all.

Peter was standing too tall. He was too self-righteous; he was too much "the leader." He had to be broken, and Jesus used Satan for that end. And so, just when Satan thought that he had Peter—there in the hall of Caiaphas, as Peter was saying, "I do not know the man," cursing and swearing—at that very moment, Jesus walked through the hall. He made eye contact with Peter. The one who said, "I have prayed for thee" gives one look and brings Peter to repentance. In that one look, he reaches in, takes away the straw, and blows away the chaff, so that the wheat will abide.

Jesus stands Satan's efforts on their head. Calvin and the Puritans rightly asserted that sometimes Christ uses Satan as a good doctor for us.[5] Where would you be without Satan's

---

5. See John Calvin, *Commentary on the Gospel According to Luke*, in

sieve—without temptation or affliction in your life? You would be spoiled and self-sufficient. But Romans 8:28 is indeed true: "All things work together for good to them that love God, to them who are the called according to his purpose." Even Satan's attempts to destroy us will be used to help us along in our spiritual maturation. This is our comfort: that Christ out-desires, out-demands, and out-prays Satan.

Your divine advocate, the ever-blessed Immanuel, pleads for you on stronger grounds and with stronger claims than the devil's, so that your faith will not fail. That word for *fail* in the Greek is a wonderful word, *ekleipó*, which means "to give out" or "to come to an end." It's where we get the English word *eclipse*. Jesus prays that your faith won't be eclipsed, won't fade out, won't die. You see, that's Satan's goal. Satan wants to destroy, to overturn, so that everything of saving grace dies within you. "Satan," Jesus is saying, "I'll let you destroy much within my people. I'll let you destroy their self-confidence, their fleshly expectations, their fleshly holiness, their fleshly pride, their fleshly wisdom, even their fleshly prayers. All that dirt must fall through the sieve. But, Satan, there is one thing I won't let you destroy: I won't let you destroy *their faith*. That faith is the noble grace by which they are united to me, and you will never sever that tie, Satan. You cannot destroy the faith that works by love, the faith that produces hope, the faith that is the heart of true godliness, the faith that cleaves and clings to me and hangs on my promises. Satan, you won't destroy Peter's faith."

What do we learn from this? As the Heidelberg Catechism says, "We are so weak in ourselves that we cannot stand

---

Calvin's Commentaries, vol. 17, *Harmony of Matthew, Mark, Luke, John 1–11* (repr., Grand Rapids: Baker, 2005), 217.

[even for] a moment."[6] But we also learn that we have an intercessor in heaven—one who keeps the feet of his saints, who removes the straw and the chaff, who preserves us even to the end. And the gates of hell will not prevail—not against a single believer (see Matt. 16:18). Reader, if you are a believer, know that your faith will never fail. It may grow weak, and at times you may not exercise it well (or may exercise it hardly at all), but it will never die—because you belong to Christ.

Ebenezer Erskine, an elderly minister who was one of the fathers of the Secession movement in Scotland, once visited a woman in his congregation who was dying. In those days, pastors often lovingly tested their own people, even when their health was failing; so Erskine said to her, "My friend, are you ready to die?"

"Oh, yes, I'm ready to go."

"On what grounds are you ready to go?"

"Well, I'm in the hands of Christ."

"But aren't you afraid you will fall through his fingers?"

"Oh, not at all."

"Why not?"

"Because of what you told us, Pastor. You said that we are part of his body. We *are* his finger, so how can we fall through?"[7]

Kingly Commission

Jesus then says something wonderful: "And when thou art converted, strengthen thy brethren" (v. 32). Our Lord provides not only prophetic admonition and priestly intercession

6. Heidelberg Catechism, answer 127.

7. See Samuel McMillan, *The Beauties of Ebenezer Erskine*, rev. ed. (Grand Rapids: Reformation Heritage Books, 2001), xlv–xlvi.

to meet our needs but also issues a kingly commission. Notice that Jesus doesn't say "*if* thou art" but "*when* thou art." He says "when," for he knows that it's going to happen—because he's the one who's going to make it happen. "Where the word of a king is, there is power" (Eccl. 8:4).

"*When* thou hast repented" is what the original Greek is saying here. That is, "When thou art turned around again, Peter, strengthen thy brethren." Jesus will effect this repentance with one look. Christ and his counterclaim gain the victory over Satan. J. P. Lange says, "The holy supplication of mercy countervails before God the daring appeal of the accuser."[8] Peter would never have repented if left to himself—but now he goes out and weeps bitterly. Now God can use him.

When the risen Christ meets with Peter privately, all that the Bible says about it is "The Lord has risen indeed, and has appeared to Simon!" (Luke 24:34 ESV). Have you ever had communion with the Lord that goes beyond words? Have you ever tried to tell someone about it, but it just seems so shallow and so hollow compared to the reality of what you've enjoyed? How the disciples must have embraced one another. Oh, the kindness of Christ! "But go, tell his disciples and Peter that he is going before you to Galilee" (Mark 16:7 ESV). *And Peter.* Peter didn't even think that he was a disciple anymore! He thought he had forfeited everything. "No," Jesus declares— "tell him that he is included."

And then Christ meets them in Galilee and restores Peter publicly. What a great reminder that when Christ does a work, he does a *full* work: "Simon, son of Jonas, lovest thou me more than these?" (John 21:15). Jesus gives him a battery of three questions, and each time Peter responds, "Yea, Lord;

8. See John Peter Lange on Luke 22:32, in *Lange's Commentary on the Holy Scriptures*, ed. Philip Schaff (repr., Grand Rapids: Zondervan, 1978).

thou knowest that I love thee." He's humbled—broken. And Jesus says to him, "Feed my sheep." It's as if to say, "Peter, now that you're broken and restored, now that you know your own frailty, now you can minister to the strong *and* to the weak."

Now I can use you, Peter! And I give you a kingly commission: go out and minister to the babes in grace, and the adolescents in grace, and the advanced in grace. Peter, now that you're broken, you will be fruitful. God often uses those people the most whom he has brought through much suffering and many trials. As A. W. Tozer writes, "If God has singled you out to be a special object of His grace you may expect Him to honor you with stricter discipline and greater suffering than less favored ones are called upon to endure."[9]

"Go strengthen your brethren, Peter." But how do you strengthen your brethren? Consider this: who stood up on the day of Pentecost to strengthen his brethren, when the church was thrown back on its heels by various accusations? Simon Peter. Although he stumbled once or twice again in the book of Acts, for much of that book we see Peter (together with Paul) in a leadership role once again—but now as one humbled and teachable. Consider too Peter's two wonderful epistles that have been used to strengthen countless believers over the millennia. Both epistles are full of the lessons Peter learned, as we see in some of the initial words of the first:

> Blessed be the God and Father of our Lord Jesus Christ, which according to his abundant mercy hath begotten us again unto a lively hope by the resurrection of Jesus Christ from the dead, To an inheritance incorruptible, and undefiled, and that fadeth not away, reserved in heaven for you,

9. A. W. Tozer, "The Ministry of the Night," *The Editorial Voice*, *The Alliance Witness*, May 15, 1963, 2.

Who are kept by the power of God *through faith* unto salvation ready to be revealed in the last time. (1 Peter 1:3–5)

"Be sober, be vigilant," Peter says later, "because your adversary the devil, as a roaring lion, walketh about, seeking whom he may devour" (1 Peter 5:8). Where do you think the apostle learned that? Peter strengthens the brethren by warning them about the bitterness of sin—the bitterness of denying the Savior. Peter emphasizes the weakness of the flesh—he warns us about the schemes of Satan. Peter declares the love of Christ and the willingness of Christ to meet all our needs as prophet, priest, and king. And Peter teaches the joy of restoration.

Where does that leave us? The question that remains is this: do we exemplify Christ's prophetical, priestly, and kingly office in our ministry to others? The Heidelberg Catechism deals with this so beautifully when it talks about Christ's three-fold office[10] and then follows it up with what seems almost like a footnote until you realize how important it is: "Why are you called a Christian?" The answer: "Because I am a member of Christ by faith, and thus a partaker of His anointing, that I may [as prophet] confess His Name, [as priest] present myself a living sacrifice of thankfulness to Him, and [as king] with a free and good conscience fight against sin and the devil in this life, and hereafter reign with Him eternally over all creatures."[11]

Is that what we're asking God for grace to do? Are you confessing Christ's name wherever you go? Do you pray for opportunities to do that, and then do you do it? Do you lay down your life as a sacrifice—not to merit anything, but simply out of gratitude—saying, "Lord, use me"? Is that your prayer

---

10. See the Heidelberg Catechism, answer 31.
11. Heidelberg Catechism, question and answer 32.

every morning? "Help me to forget myself this morning, and let me be used by thee in whatever I do"? And are you fighting against sin—truly fighting? Are you being Christ's prophet? Christ's priest? Christ's king? What kind of witness are you showing to those around you?

Do you long to be as holy in private as you appear to be in public? Do you yearn to live to the glory of your Savior in every way? Do you strive to bear office for Christ as his prophet, priest, and king in conformity to his image? Do you yearn to glorify your precious Savior with your whole life— that Savior who meets all your needs? Is that your desire? Can those who are around you—your wife, your husband, your children, your parents, your church—say of you, "This is a man, this is a woman, who walks consistently—who walks in Christ and out of Christ and reflects Christ in this world"?

All our strength, all our hope, all our future—all of it lies in Jesus. He is the secret of perseverance. The devil does not have us in checkmate, no matter how far we've fallen or how weak we are—even if we have denied Christ's name in the hall of Caiaphas or in the halls of this world. No—by the grace of Christ we have a move to make against Satan, and that move is to repent and believe in the Son of God. Put all your trust in Christ, walk in his ways, and ask for grace to reflect him as Prophet, Priest, and King. Then Satan will never checkmate you, because you live out of one who is greater than Satan—the Prophet-Priest-King Jesus Christ, who meets all your needs. Your solution is King Jesus, for he can *never* be checkmated. If you are in him, you're safe—safe forever.

8

The Final Demise

THOMAS J. NETTLES

Revelation 20:1–3, 7–10

I THINK the "final" part of this chapter's title is appropriate, since Satan's overall demise began immediately. To some degree, Satan has always had knowledge of his demise (though I suspect he was not thoroughly convinced that it was going to work out). We have evidence in Scripture that the angels are learning about this demise, in a sense, as they go along.

I'm not going wild on angelology here; the Bible has a lot to say about the whole phenomenon of angels. We know that a general kind of assignment was given to them from the very beginning, according to Hebrews 1:13–14.

And to which of the angels has he ever said,

"Sit at my right hand
until I make your enemies a footstool for your feet"?

Are they not all ministering spirits sent out to serve for the sake of those who are to inherit salvation?

Angels were on assignment from the beginning—but that assignment might not have made a lot of sense to them. On the one hand, their own glory may have seemed greater than the glory of those who were going to be created; on the other, they might not have understood the concepts of salvation and redemption and why such things would lead to their being servants of humanity.

We see more of this in Ephesians 3, where Paul speaks about the great message he has been given and how it is working itself out:

> Of this gospel I was made a minister according to the gift of God's grace, which was given me by the working of his power. To me, though I am the very least of all the saints, this grace was given, to preach to the Gentiles the unsearchable riches of Christ, and to bring to light for everyone what is the plan of the mystery hidden for ages in God, who created all things, so that through the church the manifold wisdom of God might now be made known to the rulers and authorities in the heavenly places. (Eph. 3:7–10)

This eternal purpose—having angels be ministering spirits to those who would inherit salvation—has been realized in Christ Jesus our Lord. It was hidden in God, and now by the preaching of the gospel and the gathering of the church, this eternal purpose is being made known to rulers and authorities in the heavenly places. The angels are learning about this as they go along.

We find a similar idea in 1 Peter 1:10–12, as Peter talks about how the revealed gospel has come to the apostles:

Concerning this salvation, the prophets who prophesied about the grace that was to be yours searched and inquired carefully, inquiring what person or time the Spirit of Christ in them was indicating when he predicted the sufferings of Christ and the subsequent glories. It was revealed to them that they were serving not themselves but you, in the things that have now been announced to you through those who preached the good news to you by the Holy Spirit sent from heaven, things into which angels long to look.

This work and preaching of salvation is something that the angels are learning, and it is something that Satan apparently did not like. Therefore, as he fell and sought to destroy the plan of God by attacking God's image bearers, God announced the demise of Satan: "I will put enmity between you and the woman" (Gen. 3:15).

There will be something special about the woman in this entire affair of redemption. "But when the fullness of time had come, God sent forth his Son, *born of woman*" (Gal. 4:4). Paul also said that the woman shall be "saved through childbearing" (1 Tim. 2:15). I think there's a double meaning to that: not only does life come through the woman's pain, but also the woman, as the bearer of children, will be the one who establishes the salvation that will come from the Messiah. And so God announces to Satan, "I will put enmity between you and the woman, and between your offspring and her offspring; he shall bruise your head, and you shall bruise his heel." In other words, the seed of the woman will deal a fatal blow to Satan, who has just learned more about the mystery that was hidden since before the creation of the world.

Afflicting Job

Satan learns even more about his demise through his failure to overcome God's grace toward Job. In this account we see Satan testing the loyalty of God's people. Even in his state of greatly diminished revelation, Job had high and exalted understandings of God and trusted in him. There were many things that Job did not understand, but God never really answered his questions; instead, he began asking Job questions of his own about the earth and the stars, about ostriches and ocean monsters. "Can you deal with any of these things, Job? Can you answer any of these questions?" Job could only put his hand over his mouth. The implication, of course, is that if you cannot answer questions about the things you are able to investigate, how do you possibly hope to understand the moral purposes that God has hidden in his secret counsels?

Job showed that he was a man of true faith by repenting.

> I had heard of you by the hearing of the ear,
>   but now my eye sees you;
> therefore I despise myself,
>   and repent in dust and ashes. (Job 42:5–6)

But in this process, though it brought great angst and existential difficulties, Job asked some amazing questions and learned to think clearly about theological issues. At one point we see him ask, "If a man dies, shall he live again?" (Job 14:14). It's a rhetorical question—Job implies that a man must live again, because if righteousness has any meaning at all and yet the righteous suffer this way, it must mean that there is life after this, in which what has happened in life becomes clear.

The New Testament revelation is so absolutely clear on this idea of suffering and eternal life—of the bliss that comes with eternal life and the willingness to share the sufferings of Christ. That revelation is clear to us today, but Job doesn't have the New Testament, and so he asks questions in light of Satan's assault. "Even now, behold, my witness is in heaven, and he who testifies for me is on high" (Job 16:19). Way to go, Job! That's a wonderful testimony. Led by the Spirit, he knows that there's a mediator. And then we come to Job 19:

> For I know that my Redeemer lives,
>   and at the last he will stand upon the earth.
> And after my skin has been thus destroyed,
>   yet in my flesh I shall see God,
> whom I shall see for myself,
>   and my eyes shall behold, and not another. (vv. 25–27)

Right there, Satan should have realized that his plan was doomed. You cannot cause God's elect—those who are regenerated by the spirit of God, those upon whom God has placed his special favor—to deny him. You will only make them cling to him more dearly and know him more clearly.

Tempting Jesus

We see another element of Satan's demise in his failure to lead Christ into sin. We note that Satan used the same method against Christ that he did against Eve in the garden. But Christ did not fall for Satan's ploy; in fact, Satan set in motion the very means by which, during his earthly ministry, Christ would be prepared to be the Savior. Christ understood what Satan was doing; he saw temptation and resisted it. He saw how Satan had bound people and saw the means by which he would cast Satan out by the finger of God. Jesus affirmed the will of God even as he was being assaulted by the Evil One. This is the exact argument we find when we look to the book of Hebrews:

> In the days of his flesh, Jesus offered up prayers and supplications, with loud cries and tears, to him who was able to save him from death, and he was heard because of his reverence. Although he was a son, he learned obedience through what he suffered. (Heb. 5:7–8)

Satan was putting Christ through the very trials and temptations that he needed to experience in order to establish the principle of righteousness and therefore be qualified to be the Savior. There was never a time when Christ was not obedient. There was never a time when he made a mistake and said, "Oops. If I had obeyed there, it would have been better." No—with every step he was learning the depth of the suffering that comes with obedience. The more you are plunged into the will of God, the more you are plunged into resistance against Satan. And the more you walk in righteousness, holiness, and devotion to the will of God, the more you understand the costs.

This is why Jesus said, "If anyone would come after me, let him deny himself and take up his cross and follow me" (Mark 8:34). This is exactly what he himself was doing. The cross was always before Jesus's mind, and he knew he could not go to the cross unless he had achieved the righteousness by which we could be saved. And so, though he was a son, he learned obedience through what he suffered; and, in being made perfect, he became the source of eternal salvation to all who obey him.[1]

---

1. What does it mean that Jesus was "made perfect"? As the Son of God, he surely had no imperfection in him. Jesus was infinitely excellent, and

Again Satan failed miserably. His failure to lead our Savior into sin became the occasion by which Jesus's human nature learned every aspect, every subtlety, every deviant thought, every bit of pressure that can be brought upon people to get them to disobey God. Jesus knew that Satan was coming for his final assault, but he also knew that the devil had no claim on him (see John 14:30). In fact, he was reversing everything that Satan thought he had accomplished through his temptation of Adam and Eve.

Killing Jesus

We continue to see Satan moving toward his own demise as he tried to end the ministry of Christ through death. Satan tried to have Jesus killed early on, reasoning that if he could kill Christ before he became perfect, then Christ could not be the source of eternal salvation. I'm not sure that Satan understood all of that, but he probably had a high degree of intuition about different approaches that he needed to take to try to foil God's plan through Christ.

Herod tried to kill Jesus after his birth, and yet he did not succeed (see Matt. 2). Jesus was not meant to die at just any time in any way; there was a specific time, a specific place, and a specific moral condition to which the Son of God in his incarnation had to come before he could be the Savior.

Jesus later went to preach in his hometown, and Luke

---

all the attributes of deity were his. "He is the radiance of the glory of God and the exact imprint of his nature, and he upholds the universe by the word of his power" (Heb. 1:3). All the fullness of the Godhead dwelt in him in bodily form (see Col. 2:9). And yet his humanity still needed to be tested in order for him to come to the point of perfection and a matured righteousness.

reports that "all spoke well of him and marveled at the gracious words that were coming from his mouth" (Luke 4:22). But then Jesus continued.

> Doubtless you will quote to me this proverb, "'Physician, heal yourself.' What we have heard you did at Capernaum, do here in your hometown as well." . . . Truly, I say to you, no prophet is acceptable in his hometown. But in truth, I tell you, there were many widows in Israel in the days of Elijah, when the heavens were shut up three years and six months, and a great famine came over all the land, and Elijah was sent to none of them but only to Zarephath, in the land of Sidon, to a woman who was a widow. And there were many lepers in Israel in the time of the prophet Elisha, and none of them was cleansed, but only Naaman the Syrian. (v. 23–27)

After the people heard what Jesus said, all in the synagogue were filled with wrath. Jesus had merely outlined and explained things that are clear in Scripture. Even so, they rose up and drove him out of town, even attempting to throw him down a cliff.

"Now I've got him," Satan said. "His own town has risen up. He will die, and it will be over." But, passing through their midst, Jesus went away (see v. 30). I do not know how that happened—whether he used his deity or escaped by sheer resolve—but nevertheless he knew it was not his time to die.

Satan was failing his mission to stop the ministry of Christ through murder. After the incident at Nazareth, the Jews began seeking to kill Christ "because not only was he breaking the Sabbath, but he was even calling God his own Father, making himself equal with God" (John 5:18). They began to lay plans, waiting for the opportune moment. Ironically, the sacrifice that would end all sacrifices must itself also be offered up by the high priest.

> But one of them, Caiaphas, who was high priest that year, said to them, "You know nothing at all. Nor do you under- stand that it is better for you that one man should die for the people, not that the whole nation should perish." He did not say this of his own accord, but being high priest that year he prophesied that Jesus would die for the nation, and not for the nation only, but also to gather into one the children of God who are scattered abroad. So from that day on they made plans to put him to death. (John 11:49–53)

Jesus now comes to recognize that his work is nearly com- plete. We see an indication of this two chapters later in John: "Now before the Feast of the Passover, when Jesus knew that his hour had come to depart out of this world to the Father, having loved his own who were in the world, he loved them to the end" (John 13:1). The plot thickens in chapter 18, after Jesus speaks during his trial:

> When he had said these things, one of the officers stand- ing by struck Jesus with his hand, saying, "Is that how you answer the high priest?" Jesus answered him, "If what I said is wrong, bear witness about the wrong; but if what I said is right, why do you strike me?" Annas then sent him bound to Caiaphas the high priest. (John 18:22–24)

Jesus is then sent to Pilate, who after questioning him tells the people, "I find no guilt in him" (v. 38). Yet they called for the release of Barabbas instead. John later tells us, "The Jews cried out, 'If you release this man, you are not Caesar's friend. Everyone who makes himself a king opposes Caesar.' So when Pilate heard these words . . . he delivered him over to them to be crucified" (19:12, 16).

The priests were behind all of this—particularly Caiaphas. As for Jesus, he offered himself up according to the will of the Father (see John 17:1–2). The hour had come; Jesus offered himself as the priest, as the sacrifice, as the altar. Yet this transfer from the ceremonial priesthood to the absolute, final priesthood of Christ was done in accordance with what Caiaphas himself had said: one man must die for the nation.

Satan's failure to end the ministry of Christ by death led him all the way to the point at which Jesus himself recognized that the time had come for his death. Everything had been fulfilled, and when he died, it was as a sacrifice to deliver us from this present evil age. Satan's failure, again, sealed his final demise.

Interrupting Jesus

Satan also fails to interrupt Christ's determination to go to the cross. Matthew 16 marks the first time that Jesus announces his plan—"that he must go to Jerusalem and suffer many things from the elders and chief priests and scribes, and be killed, and on the third day be raised" (v. 21). Peter takes Jesus aside and rebukes him, and Jesus immediately responds, "Get behind me, Satan!" (Matt. 16:23). Surely he hears, in Peter's rebuke, the subtle deceit of the first temptation: "You will not surely die" (Gen. 3:4). Jesus then makes a second announcement of his impending sacrifice in Matthew 17:22 (see also Luke 9:43–45). Between these announcements we have the transfiguration, when Jesus speaks to Moses and Elijah about his departure (see Luke 9:31).

On the way up to Jerusalem, Jesus makes a third announcement (see Matt. 20:17–19; Luke 18:31–33). Prior to this, Jesus gives an exposition of the coming of the Son of Man, remarking, "But first he must suffer many things and be rejected by this generation" (Luke 17:25). Then, after Jesus's triumphal entry into Jerusalem, some Gentiles begin to ask for him.

> Now among those who went up to worship at the feast were some Greeks. So these came to Philip, who was from Bethsaida in Galilee, and asked him, "Sir, we wish to see Jesus." Philip went and told Andrew; Andrew and Philip went and told Jesus. And Jesus answered them, "The hour has come for the Son of Man to be glorified. . . .
>
> "Now is my soul troubled. And what shall I say? 'Father, save me from this hour'? But for this purpose I have come to this hour. Father, glorify your name." Then a voice came from heaven: "I have glorified it, and I will glorify it again." The crowd that stood there and heard it said that it had thundered. Others said, "An angel has spoken to him." Jesus answered, "This voice has come for your sake, not mine. Now is the judgment of this world; now will the ruler of this world be cast out. And I, when I am lifted up from the earth, will draw all people to myself." (John 12:20–23, 27–32)

Satan was unable to lead Christ astray or to make any confusion in Christ's mind about his purpose. It was for this very purpose that he had come to this hour—had finally come to the point at which he had gone into Jerusalem and had caused those religious leaders to hate him so much that they were willing to compromise any kind of integrity they might have had left. They were able to compromise any kind of honesty that might have dwelt somewhere deep in their souls, any kind of true understanding of what redemption must involve, any kind of understanding of what the prophets had said about the Messiah being the one who would bear our sins in his own body. Blinded by Satan, they were able to evacuate all that and to send him to the cross through a secular government so that Peter could say at Pentecost in Acts 2:23 that Jesus was "delivered up according to the definite plan and foreknowledge of God" while at the same time saying of those who were there that day, "You crucified and killed [him] by the hands of lawless men." They had put him to death—but it was impossible for death to keep its hold on him.

Why was it impossible? Because death has come into the world only because of sin. Death is the wages of sin. And Jesus himself bore our sins in his own body on the tree so that we, being dead to sin, might live to righteousness. And so the title of John Owen's great book should stick in our minds: *The Death of Death in the Death of Christ*. When Jesus paid the price, there was no longer any way for death to keep its hold on him or on us. So we see that Satan's final demise is coming near. It is manifest in the death of Christ.

Jesus destroyed him who has the power of death—that is, the devil. That's what we learn in Hebrews 2:14, where the writer is speaking about one of the effects of the death of Christ and about the reason he had to take on our humanity. Beginning with verse 10, we read, "For it was fitting that he, for whom and by whom all things exist, in bringing many sons to glory, should make the founder of their salvation perfect through suffering. For he who sanctifies and those who are sanctified all have one source."

That means that all have one nature. Jesus is a man, just as we are.

That is why he is not ashamed to call them brothers, saying,

> "I will tell of your name to my brothers;
>   in the midst of the congregation I will sing your
>   praise."

And again,

> "I will put my trust in him."

And again,

> "Behold, I and the children that God has given me."

Since therefore the children share in flesh and blood, he himself likewise partook of the same things, that through death he might destroy the one who has the power of death, that is, the devil, and deliver all those who through fear of death were subject to lifelong slavery. (Heb. 2:11–15)

The wages of sin is gone.

The wages of sin has been paid. Christ did it. All of those whose names are written in the Lamb's Book of Life from before the foundation of the world—who, like the rest of us who believe, were by nature children of wrath—have had their sin atoned for and had a righteousness of the law, which was lived by Christ their substitute, imputed to them. The result is that they no longer need to live in fear of death or in fear of the one who had the power of death—that is, the devil.

Who's in Charge?

Why did Satan have the power of death? God gives, and God takes away. God gives life; God takes life. Read the Old Testament and see all the various things that God does—he's the one who has the prerogative to do all these things. So how does Satan have the power of death?

Satan has the power of death because he is the very one who led Eve into disobedience—the verdict of which was "You shall surely die." Satan desired to make her think that God was more merciful than that and would not make her die, but God's Word nevertheless was true. So Satan now has what he thinks is an ace: that everyone who sins must die. He sees the truth of that played out throughout human history. He sees death taking place increasingly, and perhaps he thinks, "I still have this reality: that these people are sinners—that they deserve the verdict of death—and there's nothing God can do about it." Satan reasons, "He can't redeem them. The angels cannot rescue them from their plight, for they have fallen. Look—they sinned. God said so. He said, 'In the day you eat thereof, you shall surely die.'"

It's not that Satan controls who lives and who dies. It's that he thinks that, because God is always true to his promises, he can hold the Word of God before God himself and say, "This is what you declared would happen and must happen." But God has a wisdom that Satan cannot foresee—that the redemptive purpose of God comes out in these interesting and sometimes baffling providential arrangements. And now this deeper mystery, from before the beginning of time, has come to pass: the death of the Son of God, who took our nature and was made like his brethren in everything. In doing that, Jesus has fulfilled the particular verse that Satan has clung to as his ace in the hole—the verse he's been holding before God: they sinned, they must die. Jesus has fulfilled that verse by bearing our sin in his own body on the tree. And in doing that, he destroyed him who has the power of death.

So God placed all things under his feet. When he died and rose again, it was impossible for death to keep its hold on him. In Ephesians 1:19, Paul writes of this kind of power—"the immeasurable greatness of his power toward us who believe." It is this power, this might, that was wrought in Christ when God "raised him from the dead and seated him at his right hand in the heavenly places, far above all rule and authority and power and dominion, and above every name that is named, not only in this age but also in the one to come" (Eph. 1:20–21). God has put all things under Christ's feet for the church.

All things have been placed under the feet of Christ. He has defeated all these foes. He has rescued us. Colossians 1 says that God has delivered us "from the domain of darkness and transferred us to the kingdom of his beloved Son" (v. 13). We have been rescued from the prince of the power of the air, the spirit that now works in the sons of disobedience, and we have been raised with Christ. Instead of being captive to the prince of the power of the air, we are now seated in the heavenly places in Christ. We no longer lie at Satan's disposal, for him to do with us as he sees fit.

John makes a very succinct statement about the relationship of the redeemed to Satan. He says, "We know that everyone who has been born of God does not keep on sinning, but he who was born of God"—that is, the Son of God himself, the eternally generated Son of God—"protects him, and the evil one does not touch him. We know that we are from God, and the whole world lies in the power of the evil one" (1 John 5:18–19). What a radical distinction there is now between those who have benefited from the death of Christ and those who have preferred the way of the world. The whole world lies in the power of the Evil One, but he who is born of God knows that God protects him and the Evil One does not touch him. We no longer lie at the disposal of Satan, placidly in his arms to do with us as he sees fit.

As Paul contemplates all the evil and suffering and Satan's active engagement in our world, he talks to Christians in Romans 16:20 and says that God will soon crush Satan under our feet. And of course, who can forget the reality of Paul's great confidence, which resulted from the eternal covenant of redemption that was revealed to him, when he says,

> We know that for those who love God all things work together for good, for those who are called according to his purpose. For those whom he foreknew he also predestined to be conformed to the image of his Son, in order that he might be the firstborn among many brothers. And those whom he predestined he also called, and those whom he called he also justified, and those whom he justified he also glorified. (Rom. 8:28–30)

Paul then continues,

> What then shall we say to these things? If God is for us, who can be against us? He who did not spare his own Son but gave him up for us all, how will he not also with him graciously give us all things? Who shall bring any charge against God's elect? It is God who justifies. (vv. 31–33)

If anyone could charge us, God could charge us. But in fact he is the one who justifies. "Who is he that condemns?" Well, if anyone could condemn us, it would be the Son of God, who was appointed to come and bear our sin. But the

Son of God himself, Christ Jesus, is the one who died—"more than that, who was raised, who is at the right hand of God, who indeed is interceding for us" (v. 34). Paul continues:

> Who shall separate us from the love of Christ? Shall tribulation, or distress, or persecution, or famine, or nakedness, or danger, or sword? As it is written,
>
> "For your sake we are being killed all the day long;
>> we are regarded as sheep to be slaughtered." (vv. 35–36)

Paul, quoting here from Psalm 44, is referencing a time of great suffering in Israel, when it appears that, in the strange providence of God, there was no one to come to the people's rescue. God's people—God's covenant people—were like sheep to be slaughtered.

But Paul looks at this and sees it in the context of the completed redemption—and he gives a loud "No!" because he's saying, "That's not the final story." Redemption is accomplished. "'For your sake we are being killed all the day long; we are regarded as sheep to be slaughtered.' No, in all these things we are more than conquerors" (vv. 36–37). That's a much different story from ending with "We're just like sheep to be slaughtered."

> No, in all these things we are more than conquerors through him who loved us. For I am sure that neither death nor life, nor angels nor rulers, nor things present nor things to come, nor powers, nor height nor depth, nor anything else in all creation, will be able to separate us from the love of God in Christ Jesus our Lord. (vv. 37–39)

The End of the Story

Jesus has destroyed him who has the power of death. And in Revelation 20, we do indeed see a clear, straightforward statement of the finality of the demise of Satan. But we begin to see the implosion of Satan's kingdom even earlier. In Revelation 17 we see the great prostitute, who leads all the nations into sexual immorality and idolatry, and the beast. "The woman that you saw is the great city that has dominion over the kings of the earth" (v. 18). The great prostitute is the one who's been the queen of all this wicked, godless cultural development—but now all of a sudden the ten horns and the beast turn on her. They hate the prostitute. They will make her desolate and naked and will devour her flesh and burn her up with fire, for God has put it into their hearts to carry out his purpose by being of one mind and handing over their royal power to the beast until the words of God are fulfilled.

So the great prostitute falls. The beast is still around; but now the great culture that has been created—the one that gives everyone food, jewels, and pleasure—begins to fragment. It begins to fall apart, and everyone is saying, "Oh, woe, woe; what is happening?" All the ships are sinking. No goods are coming in. They throw dust on their heads, and they weep and mourn, crying, "Alas! Alas! You great city, you mighty city, Babylon! For in a single hour your judgment has come" (Rev. 18:10). In a single hour, she has been laid waste. The whole world system—so haughty, so arrogant, so confident: "We are independent. We need depend on nothing. Through all our learning, all our science, all our philosophy, all our productivity, we can show that we can eliminate disease—can eliminate everything we don't like. We can pursue our pleasure at our whim." . . . That's all crashing down.

In Revelation 18:23–24 we read,

And the light of a lamp
    will shine in you no more,
and the voice of bridegroom and bride
    will be heard in you no more,
for your merchants were the great ones of the earth,
    and all nations were deceived by your sorcery.
And in her was found the blood of prophets and of saints,
    and of all who had been slain on earth.

But chapter 19 begins with great hallelujahs, and then we see a rider on a white horse. Someone once told one of my friends, "You Christians are just really strange. You have world-views on all these absolutes." My friend answered, "You think we're strange just because we believe that? Wait until I tell you that we think the whole world's going to come to an end by a rider on a white horse—like the Lone Ranger coming in!" We read, "Then I saw heaven opened, and behold, a white horse! The one sitting on it is called Faithful and True, and in righteousness he judges and makes war. His eyes are like a flame of fire" (Rev. 19:11–12).

In Revelation 20 an angel comes down from heaven and takes the dragon, "that ancient serpent, who is the devil and Satan, [binds] him for a thousand years, and [throws] him into the pit, and [shuts] it and [seals] it over him" (vv. 2–3). I don't profess to know all the details of this, and you can get in trouble if you profess to know too much—but I know that some things are clear. I know that God seals the 144,000 of the redeemed of all ages, and they are not going to fall away in all this time of tribulation. That happens throughout the world—throughout the ages. They are sealed. Their names are written in the Lamb's Book of Life. Anyone's name that is not found written in the Book of Life is thrown into the lake of fire.

Then there will be a time of judgment, and it seems that

this is a time when what Paul said in Romans 3 actually comes to pass: when every mouth is stopped and the whole world is held guilty before God (see v. 19). After Satan is cast into a pit and it is sealed, a judgment takes place. "I saw thrones, and seated on them were those to whom the authority to judge was committed. Also I saw the souls of those who had been beheaded for the testimony of Jesus and for the word of God, and those who had not worshiped the beast or its image and had not received its mark on their foreheads or their hands" (Rev. 20:4). This is happening for whatever "a thousand years" means.

After all of that judgment takes place, Satan is released; and even though everyone has consented to this judgment, Satan's power to deceive again comes to life, and he makes his allies think that they can make one more attempt to defeat the plan of God. They gather all their forces together against God. They march up over the broad plain of the earth and surround the camp of the saints and the beloved city—but fire comes down from heaven and consumes them. God fights for his people, the saints. He has defeated his enemies at the cross. He has destroyed him who has the power of death. And now his final consignment: "And the devil who had deceived them was thrown into the lake of fire and sulfur where the beast and the false prophet were, and they will be tormented day and night forever and ever" (Rev. 20:10).

Then there's a picture of the new heaven and the new earth—the new Jerusalem; the river of life. The beauty of all this for those whom God has redeemed is almost beyond description. But we are told that nothing unclean will ever enter it, nor anyone who does what is detestable or false, but only those who are written in the Lamb's Book of Life. Earlier we read, "But as for the cowardly, the faithless, the detestable, as for murderers, the sexually immoral, sorcerers, idolaters, and all liars, their portion will be in the lake that burns with fire and sulfur, which is the second death" (Rev. 21:8).

The story concludes in Revelation 22:

> Blessed are those who wash their robes, so they may have a right to the tree of life, that they may enter the city by the gates. Outside are the dogs and sorcerers, the sexually immoral and murderers, and idolaters, and everyone who loves and practices falsehood. (vv. 14–15)

We have an affirmation of the person of Christ, an affirmation of the work of the Spirit in bringing people to Christ, and an affirmation of the finality and truthfulness of these descriptions of the Word of God—an affirmation of the true apostolic authority and revelatory status of John and his writing (see vv. 16–19). "He who testifies of these things says, 'Surely I am coming soon.' Amen. Come, Lord Jesus!" (v. 20).

And then, appropriately, the whole Scripture ends with "The grace of the Lord Jesus be with all. Amen" (v. 21). Of course, this naturally leads to the following question: do you have the grace of the Lord Jesus? It's very clear from the testimony of Scripture that without the grace of the Lord Jesus, no one will escape the condemnation of Satan and of all those who have been in league with him—all those world systems that have sought to further his agenda. Everyone who has not escaped that by the grace of our Lord Jesus will be cast into that same place that was actually prepared for the devil and his angels. Those who fit within his framework, those who have followed his pattern of life, will find themselves in company with him forever. But there will be no more glee; there will be no more hope and promise that perhaps we can win. There will be no more fellowship or friendship with the drunkards. All the country songs that say, "I want to go to hell because that's where all my good friends are going to be"—that's a charade that isn't going to work out at all. No one will be a friend there.

It's not as though Satan himself is going to have power. It's not as if he's going to be gleeful over having his own domain in which he can actually recall the evil that he wants to and be happy about it. No—he himself is going to be under the wrath of God. It is a place prepared for him as an exquisite display of the holiness and justice of God—a manifestation of wrath that we cannot even conceive. Those who maintain their allegiance to his way of looking at the world will find themselves in company with him.

But the wonderful end of this book sets before us the reality that, while we're in this life, we can discover and embrace the grace of God. John ends Revelation on a triumphant note by writing, "He who testifies of these things says, 'Surely I am coming soon.'" Then the apostle, along with everyone who shares his salvation, says, "Amen. Come, Lord Jesus!" And a final word of hope: "The grace of the Lord Jesus be with all."

9

All Things New

Revelation 21:1–8

THE SCRIPTURES invite us to think about sin from two different perspectives. They invite us to think about the origin and nature of sin, about the damage that sin has done to our relationship to God, and about the seriousness of our own sinfulness before his judgment. But the Scriptures also invite the believing people of God to see the conquest and defeat of sin—and, by the power of the Holy Spirit, to see it day by day as we seek to live the Christian life.

Our enemy has been defeated, and only one question remains: what happens when sin has, once and for all, been vanquished? The book of Revelation leads us to that great climactic point.

I have little doubt that some of us are more frightened of the book of Revelation than of any other book in the Bible, and there are a variety of reasons why we are frightened to teach it and to expound it in public. Yet there is a sense in which the book of Revelation is the easiest, not the most difficult, book in the New Testament. It's easiest because it is the book in which, more than in any other, God comes down to the simplest of us. Instead of explaining the gospel to us in the great doctrinal expositions that we find, for example, in some of Paul's letters, and instead of showing us the glory of God and the glory of the gospel and the character of the Christian life and the conquest of God's grace simply by means of words, God sits down beside us in the book of Revelation as though we were his little children and says to us, "Look at the picture book that I've made for you."

Here God takes us through the teaching that he gave to the apostle John. He points to various pictures, as though we were little children who are scarcely able to understand, and says, "Do you see this? This is what I will do. Do you see these dark monsters? They are pictures of the power of sin and its influence—the power of Satan and his demons. Do you see that Lamb standing as though he had been slain? That is the one who will save the people of God from their sin, will deliver them from the power of darkness, and will bring them into the new age."

G. K. Chesterton once inscribed in a children's book,

Stand up and keep your childishness:
    Read all the pedants' screeds and strictures;
But don't believe in anything
    That can't be told in coloured pictures.[1]

1. See Alfred George Gardiner, *Prophets, Priests and Kings* (London: Alston Rivers, 1908), 327.

That's exactly what the book of Revelation is: a book of colored pictures, multicolored pictures, dramatic pictures about the power and majesty of God's victory over sin.

From another point of view, this book is almost like God's family vacation movie—full of details of incidents that, unless we're familiar with the family, may pass us by. It can also seem as though it comes to us in unedited form, full of impressions that are meant to strike even those of us who scarcely know anything about the Bible or about the history of God's people in the Bible. We find great, vivid pictures that are meant to impress on our minds great truths about the grace of God, his conquest over sin, and the great new heavens and earth that he will create, wherein his glory will be magnified and seen.

It is in this context that I want you to notice the great vision that John finally receives in Revelation 21–22. You'll see that a very interesting thing happens to him in Revelation 21:10. John tells us that one of the angels came to him and that he was carried away in the Spirit to a great, high mountain and was shown this marvelous vision that he describes at length. It's almost as though he has been given a free helicopter ride over what God is going to do. He is given a glorious aerial view that lets him see with great clarity what God plans to do in order to bring the salvation of his people to consummation.

In the first nine verses of that chapter, until this great vision unfolds before him from an aerial point of view, John gives us hints of the themes that will emerge. Then, in the verses that follow, he takes us around these different pictures of the glory of God and invites us to see what he has seen of God's power.

Three special pictures or themes emerge in Revelation 21:1–9. First, we see a picture of the experience of the people of God. John describes this in terms of a new city coming down from heaven. Second, we are given a picture of the new worship of God, which is described in terms of an amazing new temple—the tabernacle of God: "Behold, the dwelling place of God is with man" (v. 3). Finally, to give us a picture of the work of God, John shows us a new world, a new universe, a new heaven and earth that God himself will bring into being. These three pictures are simply different ways to view the great climactic and consummative work of God as he brings his people at last into the newness of his presence and shows them the majesty of his glory.

The New Bride

The first picture that John paints for us of the new city for the people of God is that of "the holy city, new Jerusalem, coming down out of heaven from God" (v. 2). It's a picture of what God does in bringing the church into being. It doesn't arise from the earth; it comes down from heaven. The church is not created by man, and it's not merely a religious society; rather, it is created by God and has a heavenly origin. Its citizens have their citizenship not upon earth but in heaven.

As John begins to unfold this vision, he shares with us his own sense of being staggered by what God is showing him. First, he's staggered because of the sheer size of the city.

> And the one who spoke with me had a measuring rod of gold to measure the city and its gates and walls. The city lies foursquare, its length the same as its width. And he measured the city with his rod, 12,000 stadia. Its length and width and height are equal. (Rev. 21:15–16)

That's about 1,500 miles from north to south, east to west, top to bottom. This great, perfect cube is so immense

that its area is like the area you would circumscribe by drawing a line from Philadelphia to Winnipeg to San Francisco to
Houston and back to Philadelphia. It would take virtually the
whole of the United States to begin to express even from one
dimension the majesty, size, and splendor of this city. Not only
that, he says, but it reaches upward as far as it reaches outward.
In this picture of immensity John is displaying the perfections
of living in the city. If people thought the United States had
everything to offer, John counters, "This *really* has everything
to offer." If there is an American dream, John notes that "this
is the great dream of the godly man that will finally be satisfied
by God's grace." It is truly awesome in its size.

But not only is John staggered because of its size; he's
even more staggered because of its beauty, which he describes
in great detail. The new Jerusalem comes down from heaven
beautifully adorned, "having the glory of God, its radiance like
a most rare jewel, like a jasper, clear as crystal" (v. 11). Then he
goes on to describe what the angel displayed to him as he was
taken around the majestic city. It is almost as though this angel
were a divinely appointed realtor sent to say to John, "Look—
look at the beauty and splendor of this place" (see vv. 18–21).
Imagine writing an advertisement for the *Philadelphia Inquirer*
for this:

> City for possession. 1,500 miles of real estate. Twelve
> gates—each huge gate guarding walls that are 144 cubits
> wide; each huge gate made of one immerse pearl. The main
> street made of solid gold; and in the middle of the main
> street, of all places, a river—the waters of life flowing—and
> in the centerpiece of the river a majestic tree of life standing
> and bestriding both sides of the river. This tree bears fruit
> every single month of the year, its leaves being for the heal-
> ing of the nations.

John simply can't get over the beauty. He struggles with language. He ransacks what he knows is beautiful in the eyes of men and women to try to express how glorious this city seems to him. But neither of these things is ultimately what most staggers him. Great in size it may be, and beautiful to behold it may be—but it's neither the size nor the beauty of the city that is its real secret. Its real secret is its *identity*.

You remember how John begins to explain to us what that identity is? He says there are twelve gates of the city and twelve foundations to the city. On the gates are written the names of the tribes of Israel, and on the foundations are the names of the twelve apostles of the Lamb. You see what he's saying? He is saying that this city is really a picture of the people of God in every generation: the Old Testament period represented by the twelve tribes of Israel, and the New Testament period represented by the names of the twelve apostles. As we look at this city closely and examine its details, we see it strangely transformed from being an inanimate city to being an infinite multitude of men and women that no man can number, drawn from every age and period in the history of God's redemptive work, gathered together and adorned in splendor before the presence of the great God and Savior. God is fulfilling the ancient covenant promise that they would be his people and he would be their God.

What is supremely important is that the city shone, "having the glory of God" (v. 11), and that it came down "prepared as a bride adorned for her husband" (v. 2). That's the heart of what John wants us to see. That's the explanation for the splendor and adornment of the city of God. This bride shines with the glory of God and is adorned by the glory of God to be presented to her husband—the Lamb of God, the Son of God, the Christ of God. All this beauty, all this majesty, all this glory is bestowed on the bride not for her own sake but so that she may be beautiful, glorious, acceptable, and lovely in the eyes of the Bridegroom—in order that he may look upon her and be satisfied absolutely with her beauty.

The apostle Paul says that "woman is the glory of man" (1 Cor. 11:7). This is the mystery that God's Word foreshadows in the first marriage in the garden of Eden, when the Lord brings the woman to the man and gives her to him. This is what is portrayed in every true marriage ceremony—what is illustrated in every true Christian marriage. The whole of marital history points forward to this great consummation when, down the aisle from heaven on the arm of the heavenly Father, will come the bride of his beloved Son, adorned as a bride for her husband.

> The bride eyes not her garment,
> but her dear bridegroom's face;
> I will not gaze at glory,
> but on my King of grace;
> not at the crown he giveth,
> but on his piercèd hand;
> the Lamb is all the glory
> of Emmanuel's land.[2]

That's what John is showing us: this glorious picture of the city of God, the people of God, as the bride of Christ. This is the picture of what we shall be. If there is an ounce of true spiritual reality in our hearts, there ought to arise, in response to this picture, a sigh of longing for that day. There arises from the consummation of this picture a sense that we ourselves will say, as Adam said in the garden of Eden, "At last, at last, at last"; for even that, John is teaching us, will be but a faint echo of the words that will issue from the lips of our blessed

2. Anne R. Cousin, "The Sands of Time Are Sinking," 1857.

145

redeemer, Jesus Christ—"At last. This is bone of my bone, flesh of my flesh"—as he embraces us forever as his bride.

The New Temple

While the first picture is that of a city that turns into a bride—the bride of the Lamb—the second picture is of a temple coming down for the worship of God. "And I heard a loud voice from the throne saying, 'Behold, the dwelling place of God is with man. He will dwell with them, and they will be his people, and God himself will be with them as their God'" (v. 3).

But then, as John is taken on this exploratory picture of the great city, inevitably he looks around for the temple. Where, in the midst of this majestic, glorious, vast city, will he find the place where God is to be worshiped? He goes along the main street of God. He sees the rivers of water. He sees the majestic Tree of Life and its leaves that bear fruit and heal the nations. Yet the question perplexes him—where is the temple where God is to be worshiped? John tells us, after his exploration, "And I saw no temple in the city, for its temple is the Lord God the Almighty and the Lamb" (v. 22). Having introduced us to our betrothal to Jesus Christ, our marriage to Jesus Christ, and our presence with Jesus Christ, John introduces us to the activity in which we will be engaged: the worship and adoration and service of Jesus Christ.

John has much to say about this worship, and this is vital for us to grasp if our worship now is to be a reflection *of* and a desire *for* the worship that is yet to be. John stresses, for example, its purity: "[The city] gates will never be shut by day—and there will be no night there" (v. 25). There is no need to protect this city. None will be banished from it. None who can defile will ever enter into it. In previous chapters, John has

146

already painted pictures—terrible pictures in many ways—of the banishment of sinners from the presence of God and of the banishment of Satan and his hosts from all of their activity of seeking to destroy the people of God. But now God has closed off his people, and there is no more risk that anything impure will ever enter.

Think of it: no fear of sin; no presence of sin; no fear of temptation; no cause of temptation; no shame that will paralyze the worship of God's people; no anxiety about the future, and our future falling, that will ever perplex us. Nothing that is impure will enter in—nothing that can deceive. There will be no hypocrisy. There will be no speaking out of both sides of the mouth in the worship of God. All will be refined in the presence of the Lamb and of the Lord.

John paints a picture of men and women who are, at last, free to worship and serve God without the pain of the downward drag of the world, the flesh, and the devil. If, for instance, we as city dwellers go out into the country in spring or in autumn, simply to be free of the pollution that has clogged our lungs, we finally gain the opportunity to breathe in what we may call "God's pure air." As we stand and behold the beauty of his creation and take in deep breaths of our longed-for fresh air, we say, "Oh, isn't it glorious? Isn't this how it should be?" So it will be, says John. We will say to one another, "Isn't it glorious to be freed, finally, from the very presence of sin and to be free to worship God?"

In addition to the purity of the worship in the new Jerusalem, John sees also the internationality of the worship there. "By [the city's] light will the nations walk, and the kings of the earth will bring their glory into it" (v. 24). It's a picture that John has already unfolded earlier in Revelation: a picture of the great representatives of multitudes that no man can number, from north and south and east and west—from every tribe and tongue and people and nation. The sheer internationality of the grace of God, and its manifestations in a variety of different cultures, will all be brought together. All the ransomed hosts of Christ from every tongue, people, tribe, and nation will be gathered together in the one great city, reflecting the glory of the Lord and of the Lamb.

All the fragments of the jigsaw puzzle of God's grace in history will finally be put into place in all their multicolored hues of glory. The worship there will be tinged with everything that has been marked by the grace of God and the lives of his people, who come from every tribe and tongue and nation. I wonder what it will mean, then, to apply the regulative principle of worship to public worship: how glorious it will be, how magnificent it will be, to hear the songs of the nations all praising the Lord and praising the Lamb in the power of the Holy Spirit.

We are told, John says, that the Lamb and the Lord are themselves the temple. But do you notice where they are? John says in Revelation 22:3, "No longer will there be anything accursed, but the throne of God and of the Lamb will be in it, and his servants will worship him." And John also mentions "the river of the water of life, bright as crystal, flowing from the throne of God and of the Lamb" (v. 1). This appears to be a picture of the presence and power of the Holy Spirit, constantly refreshing the people of God, constantly energizing them as he brings them to kneel before the throne of the Lamb, to kiss the Son and live, to bow before him in their worship and their adoration, and to yield to him everything that is theirs. Never will it be said more truly by any bride than it will be said on that day: "With our body we thee worship and adore."

John is beginning to share what it was that the Old Testament psalmist desired when he longed, in the experience of worship, for the Lord to be enthroned upon the praises of his people (see Ps. 22:3). We know something of that, in worship, when we say that God has come down among his people. In his letter to the Corinthians, Paul expressed his longing that even an unbeliever would come into their church and be so struck by the sense of the presence of God that he would fall down on his knees and say, "Surely God is among you" (see 1 Cor. 14:25). The people convey this sense by their praising hearts—by the melodies and the songs and the adoration—so that they lift up Jehovah upon the throne of their own praises and exalt him, that he might be high and lifted up and that his glory might fill the place where they meet.

John is saying that this ancient longing of the psalmist will be consummated here in the heavenly city and in the heavenly temple, because the Lord and the Lamb will be seated upon the throne and the servants of God will serve him in priestly worship and ministry.

The New World

First, John pictures a city that comes down and becomes a bride prepared for Christ. Then he draws a picture of a temple that has no walls, but in the midst of it stands a throne where men and women worship the Lord and the Lamb. Finally he provides a picture of a new world that displays the work of God. Do you see what happens in these chapters? It is something very striking. If you have ever read through the whole book of Revelation at a sitting—which is the way, really, to read it—one thing you may notice is that, throughout the book, God hardly ever speaks a word.

However, God does speak in Revelation 21:3: "Behold, the dwelling place of God is with man. He will dwell with them, and they will be his people, and God himself will be with them as their God." What is God going to do? John tells us that a new heaven and a new earth will be brought into being, and the first heaven and the first earth will pass away. It's the consummation of what Paul longed for when he said that we have a sense that the whole creation is groaning and travailing together (see Rom. 8:22)—longing for the day when the sons of God will be brought into their own, longing for the day of the marriage supper of the Lamb. In that day, everything will be changed, refined, transformed, and renewed. As the people of God will have resurrection bodies, so the world that God has created will become a resurrection universe. There, righteousness and peace will dwell, the lion will lie down with the lamb, and there will be no more sea.[3]

What will characterize this new heaven and new earth? "Oh," John marvels, "no longer will there be anything accursed, but the throne of God and of the Lamb will be in it, and his servants will worship him" (22:3). Why will there be no more curse? Because the Lamb who was accursed for our sakes will stand in the center of the throne. There will be no more curse, because on his hands, his side, and his forehead, there will be the faint reminders of the suffering he endured to bear the judgment curse of God and to exhaust the judgment curse of God against our sin. Is it any wonder that the book ends this way, in Revelation 22:20–21?

> He who testifies to these things says, "Surely I am coming soon." Amen. Come, Lord Jesus!
> The grace of the Lord Jesus be with all. Amen.

---

3. In the language of Revelation, this means there will be no more place from which the horrid monsters of the powers of darkness may emerge to threaten the people of God.

ALLIANCE®
OF CONFESSING EVANGELICALS

What is the Alliance?

The Alliance of Confessing Evangelicals is a coalition of confessional pastors, scholars, and churchmen who hold to the historic creeds and confessions of the Reformed faith and who proclaim biblical doctrine in order to foster a Reformed awakening in today's church. Our members join for gospel proclamation, biblically sound confessional doctrine, fostering of reformation, and the glory of God. We work and serve the church through broadcasting, events, and publishing.

The work started in broadcasting beginning with *The Bible Study Hour* with James Boice. Subsequent broadcasts are *Every Last Word* featuring Philip Ryken, *Mortification of Spin* with Carl Trueman, Todd Pruitt, and Aimee Byrd, *No Falling Word* with Liam Goligher, *Theology on the Go* with Jonathan Master and James Dolezal, and *Dr. Barnhouse & the Bible* with Donald Barnhouse. These broadcasts air throughout North America and online at AllianceNet.org.

Place for Truth is our online magazine—a free "go-to" theological resource. *reformation21* provides cultural and church critique. *The Shepherd Leader* is a resource for pastors and church leaders. *Meet the Puritans* shares the theology and writing of the Puritans with a modern audience. Our online daily devotionals include *Think and Act Biblically*, also from Dr. Boice, and MatthewHenry.org, a resource fostering biblical prayer.

Our events include the Philadelphia Conference on Reformed Theology, the oldest continuing national Reformed conference in North America, and regional events such as the Quakertown Conference on Reformed Theology. Pastors' events, such as reformation societies, continue to encourage, embolden, and equip church leaders in pursuit of reformation in the church.

Alliance publishing includes books from a list of trustworthy authors, with titles such as *Entering God's Rest, Knowing the Trinity, Zeal for Godliness, Our Creed,* and more. We also offer a vast list of affordable booklets, as well as e-books such as *The Authority of Scripture* and *Why and How to Study the Bible.*

The Alliance further seeks to encourage sound biblical doctrine by offering a wide variety of CD and MP3 resources featuring Alliance broadcast speakers and many other nationally recognized pastor-theologians at ReformedResources.org.

For more on the Alliance, visit AllianceNet.org.

Did you find this book helpful?
Consider writing a review online.
We appreciate your feedback!

Or write to P&R at editorial@prpbooks.com
with your comments. We'd love to hear from you.

This book takes dead aim at the heart of ongoing sin. Drawing from two masterful works by John Owen, Kris Lundgaard offers insight, encouragement, and hope for overcoming the enemy within.

"A solid reminder that apart from the grace of God we are far weaker than we can imagine—but greater is he that is in us than he that is in the world."
> —**Bryan Chapell**, Author of *Holiness by Grace: Delighting in the Joy That Is Our Strength*

"Fresh, contemporary, highly readable. Every Christian who is serious about holiness should read this book."
> —**Jerry Bridges**, Author of *Respectable Sins: Confronting the Sins We Tolerate*